THE BEST OF The **MAILBOX**® Magazine

Smith

Authors

GRADES 1–3

P9-CBV-342

Introduce your students to 27 of today's most acclaimed children's book authors and enrich your curriculum with teacher-tested ideas based on their books. *The Best Of* The Mailbox® *Authors* spotlights authors whose works have proven to be enduring favorites with children and includes literature-based teaching units—selected from issues of *The Mailbox*® magazine primary edition, published between 1991 and 1998—that provide an abundance of natural connections to content-area learning.

In each author feature you'll find the following:

• Background information to introduce the author
• Brief summaries of several of the author's books
• Cross-curricular classroom activities connected to the featured books
• A list of additional books by the author

Note To The Teacher: *Unless indicated, all of the books featured in this fabulous resource were in print at the time the original magazine articles were published. We've taken care to choose featured units and books for this resource which are currently in print, but cannot guarantee that every book featured will remain in print. Should you have any trouble locating any of the titles featured herein, check with your media specialist.*

Editor:
Kim T. Griswell

Artists:
Marilynn G. Barr, Pam Crane, Teresa R. Davidson, Susan Hodnett,
Mary Lester, Rebecca Saunders, Barry Slate, Donna Teal

Cover Artist:
Kimberly Richard

©1999 by THE EDUCATION CENTER, INC.
All rights reserved.
ISBN #1-56234-316-5

Manufactured in the United States
10 9 8 7 6 5 4 3 2 1

Table Of Contents

Jan Brett

Fairy Tales, Folklore, And Faraway Places

ideas by Karen P. Shelton

In her childhood Jan Brett often retreated into the pages of beautiful picture books and dreamed of becoming an illustrator. Years later, as a student at the Boston Museum School, she spent hours in the Museum of Fine Arts. Today she finds inspiration in the stories she heard as a child, the art and architecture of foreign countries, and the people and pets in her life.

One of Jan Brett's favorite animals is the hedgehog. Part of his appeal, she believes, is his nice shape and distinctive scuttle-like gait. But she is also attracted by his gentle and determined demeanor. When reading Jan Brett's books, be sure to look for her friend the hedgehog since he appears in several of her works.

Every book by Jan Brett reflects her unwavering attention to detail and passion for authenticity. In a world in which far too many things seem mundane, mass-produced, and sacrificed for the bottom line, Jan Brett infuses her books with the painstaking care of a master craftsman.

Use the suggestions that follow (on pages 4–7) to introduce your youngsters to several of Jan Brett's books and to involve them in related activities.

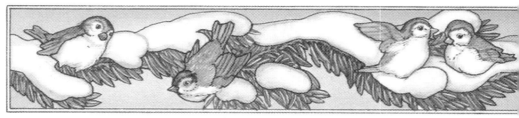

Beauty And The Beast
Published by Clarion

Jan Brett struck the perfect balance of text and art in her retelling of the fairy tale *Beauty And The Beast.* Read the story aloud. Then ask youngsters if they knew in advance how the story would end. Encourage them to reexamine the book for visual clues to the true identities of the palace characters. (Many clues are found in the tapestries.) Then ask student volunteers to talk about times when they have felt judged on the basis of their appearance. As a group, brainstorm special qualities that a person can have other than good looks. Ask your youngsters to name some ways that they have gotten to know the hidden inner strengths of other people.

Encourage students to bring various versions of *Beauty And The Beast* to school. Have them read and compare the books to determine the differences and similarities. Then, to determine the most popular version, have each student indicate his preference on a graph by using a rose sticker. Ask students to justify their choices.

Before tucking this book on a classroom shelf, have youngsters locate the hedgehog in your copy of *Beauty And The Beast.*

The Twelve Days of Christmas
Published by G. P. Putnam's Sons

Hoping to inject new vibrancy into a traditional English carol, Jan Brett created her own version of *The Twelve Days Of Christmas.* But she also injected this edition with more substance than first meets the eye.

After reading the story aloud to your youngsters or singing it with them, project the illustrations onto a screen using an opaque projector and reexamine them as a group. Point out that 11 of the two-page illustrations include the words *Merry Christmas* written in different languages. Encourage youngsters to learn to say Merry Christmas in a foreign language with the help of an older relative or friend. Have pairs (or small groups) of more advanced students select a spelling of Merry Christmas from the book to investigate. Ask students to determine the language from which their spelling comes and how the accompanying illustrations relate to the lands in which this language is spoken.

Before putting this book on your classroom library shelf for everyone to enjoy, be sure to mention that Jan Brett whimsically sees herself as the goose in the white babushka (folded kerchief head covering) in the illustration for "Six geese a-laying."

4

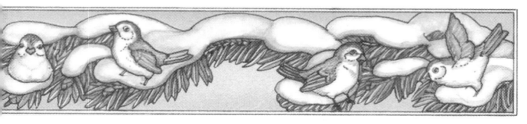

The Owl And The Pussycat
Written by Edward Lear
Published by G. P. Putnam's Sons

Jan Brett wanted to illustrate Edward Lear's "The Owl And The Pussycat," because she loved it as a child, as did her own daughter. She chose the island of Martinique—also known as the Isle of Flowers—as the setting for her version of "The Owl And The Pussycat." Since the people of Martinique make an everyday practice of decorating with flowers, a flower is tucked into every two-page spread of the book. After reading the story aloud and finding Martinique on a map, have students locate the names of various flowers shown in the book by using library references. Or have students use references from the library to identify the underwater creatures or the shells shown.

When visiting Martinique in preparation for this book, Jan Brett discovered that the people of Martinique paint their house and boats using bright colors and fanciful combinations. Ask each youngster to sketch and paint a colorful Caribbean house after closely examining the houses in the book. Have him include himself in the picture and glue on crumpled tissue-paper squares for flowers.

Berlioz The Bear
Published by G. P. Putnam's Sons

The dedication in this Reading Rainbow Book is simply "To Joe." Joseph Hearne airbrushes the backgrounds of Jan Brett's books with a fine spray of paint. But Joe is much more than an artistic accomplice. He's Brett's husband, the model for Berlioz, and probably her number one fan. Joe is a bassist in the Boston Symphony Orchestra. Together the couple travels the world. Not too long ago, they visited Bavaria where Jan found the inspiration for the scenes and costumes in *Berlioz The Bear*.

If you're planning a musical outing, use *Berlioz The Bear* to pique students' interest, or use it as an amusing follow-up to a music-related field trip. At the conclusion of the book, ask students to determine what musical piece Berlioz played as an encore. Play a recording of Rimsky-Korsakov's "Flight Of The Bumblebee," and have youngsters discuss their interpretations of the music.

Take another look at the illustrations of the orchestra in *Berlioz The Bear*. A group of musicians posed as models for the scenes in the book. Ask your students if they can imagine the models' reactions to the finished illustrations.

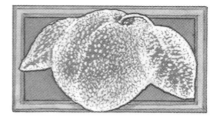

The Mitten
Published by G. P. Putnam's Sons

Three teachers mentioned to Jan Brett that she should adapt and illustrate the Ukrainian folktale *The Mitten.* And what a splendid idea that turned out to be! Before she began working, a Ukrainian woman translated different versions of the story into English for her. At the Ukrainian Museum in New York City, Jan learned that many children in the Ukraine wear hand-me-downs. So she decided to outfit the child in the story with oversized clothes. She also learned that it's a Ukrainian custom to hang a water jug on a fence so that passersby can get a drink and that a stork's nest on a cottage roof is believed to bring good luck. After reading the story aloud, help students locate the Ukraine on a map. Then explain the significance of the jug and the stork's nest, and have youngsters reexamine the book to look for these elements.

Traditionally, variations of this story have centered around mittens or pots that accommodated the animals. Ask your youngsters to think of other things that could have sheltered several animals. Also invite students to brainstorm catastrophes other than a bear's sneeze that could have sent the animals flying everywhere. Have students dictate and illustrate a new version of this old, old tale.

What ever happened to those teachers who suggested that Jan write this book? Well, whenever a child opens Jan Brett's *The Mitten,* he can read their names on the dedication page. Tad Beagley, the fourth person to whom the book is dedicated, was the model for Nicki.

Annie And The Wild Animals
Published by Houghton Mifflin

If your youngsters are studying the seasons, *Annie And The Wild Animals* is an excellent read-aloud choice. In this story, Annie's cat becomes unusually antisocial and wanders off into the wilderness, leaving Annie lonely indeed. Observant readers can scan the detailed borders to find out what's happening in the woods around Annie as she tries to lure another animal for a pet.

After reading the book aloud, have youngsters closely examine the pictures in the first half of the book. Ask them to describe the setting as you note their comments on a chalkboard. Then have them describe the changes in the setting as they examine the second half of the book. Make a separate list of these comments. Ask student volunteers to label each list with the appropriate season name.

Trouble With Trolls
Published by G. P. Putnam's Sons

Have you noticed that those little troll dolls have begun to reappear after many, many years in hiding? Jan Brett's newest book is about a little girl who is confronted by trolls (no relation to the plastic-and-fur ones) that want her dog for a pet. With creativity and spunk, she helps the trolls find the perfect pet—and it's not her dog. As you're reading this book, be on the lookout for one of Jan Brett's favorite animals! When you've read the story aloud, provide fake fur scraps and construction paper, and ask students to create trolls of their own. Encourage them to make pets for their trolls too.

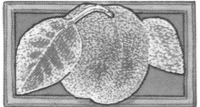

The Wild Christmas Reindeer
Published by G. P. Putnam's Sons

Jan Brett was having some trouble with her horse, Westminster, about the time that she had decided to write a book about the North Pole. She noticed that when she was demanding with "Westy," he tended to balk. But when she spoke calmly to him, he was much more likely to comply. With a change of setting and characters, Jan Brett converted her own real-life experiences into the story of a reindeer handler named Teeka. In preparation for doing the artwork, Jan visited Norway where a stave church inspired her design of the reindeer bar. She also photographed some very affectionate caribou at the University of Maine in preparation for illustrating the book.

The first date that appears in the book's borders is December 1. That's not only an appropriate starting point for a Christmas book; it's also Jan Brett's birthday. Another look at the borders of this book reminds us of the appeal of handcrafted gifts. Call your youngsters' attention to the things that the elves are making. Ask them to vote for their favorite elf project of those shown in the book. Then assist students as they create a simplified version of the most popular project. Photograph students at work and display the pictures in a pretty tower cutout similar to a tower in the book's borders.

Other Books Written Or Retold And Illustrated by Jan Brett

Fritz And The Beautiful Horses
(Houghton Mifflin)

Goldilocks And The Three Bears
(G. P. Putnam's Sons)

The First Dog
(Harcourt Brace Jovanovich)

Other Books Illustrated by Jan Brett

Happy Birthday, Dear Duck
by Eve Bunting (Clarion)

Scary, Scary Halloween
by Eve Bunting (Clarion)

The Mother's Day Mice
by Eve Bunting (Clarion)

Noelle Of The Nutcracker
by Pamela Jane (Houghton Mifflin)

The Valentine Bears
by Eve Bunting (Clarion)

St. Patrick's Day In The Morning
by Eve Bunting (Clarion)

Jan Brett welcomes and replies to mail from teachers and children. As a courtesy to the author, it's best to send either one letter from the class or to package individual student letters in a single large envelope.

Jan Brett
132 Pleasant Street
Norwell, MA 02061

Thank You, Eric Carle

When we asked teachers for their best activities to supplement Eric Carle books, we had to get very busy opening mail! The fantastic response was, no doubt, a testament to the value of Carle's books. Pick and choose from among these classroom-tested suggestions to complement your favorite Carle books.

Getting To Know The Man Behind It All

Millions of children, parents, teachers and librarians the world over know and love the books of Eric Carle. And most of them suspect that Eric Carle is a man of great warmth and generosity, an artist of tremendous depth. *The Eric Carle Picture Writer Video* will confirm these very thoughts. For 27 minutes, step into the wonderful world of Eric Carle. Discover how he gets his ideas, learn his secrets and fondest childhood memories, and watch as his Very Hungry Caterpillar is born from brilliantly painted tissue-paper collages. Gentle, entertaining, informative, and inspiring, this video presentation is a must for your Eric Carle collection. (If not available locally, contact Philomel Books [1-800-631-8571].)

Penning Your Thoughts

Here's a fun way to incorporate journal writing into your author study. For added writing motivation, have students create journal covers, featuring collage artwork that mimics Carle's style. In preparation for this activity, have students analyze and discuss illustrations from several of Carle's books. Explain that he paints on tissue paper with acrylic paint, cuts out shapes from the paper, uses rubber cement to attach the shapes to the page, and adds details using crayon here and there. To begin this activity, have each youngster create two finger paintings. Then have him cut desired shapes from his dried finger paintings and use rubber cement to attach them to a 12" x 18" sheet of construction paper that has been folded in half to create a 9" x 12" folder. Have students use markers to personalize their covers and add desired details; then unfold the covers and laminate them for durability. Refold the covers, staple a supply of writing paper inside each, and the journals are ready. Follow up each presentation of an Eric Carle book with journal-writing time. If desired, ask students to write why they liked the story, describe their favorite parts of the story, explain what they learned from the story, or create their own versions of the story. The writing possibilities are endless!

Patty Cheek—Gr. 2, Camp Creek School, Lilburn, GA

The Tiny Seed

• Try this tasty follow-up activity after reading aloud *The Tiny Seed.* To make an edible sunflower, use a jar lid to make a circular imprint on a slice of bread; then cut out the resulting shape. Spread a layer of peanut butter on the circle of bread and sprinkle it with sunflower kernels. Add a celery stick stem and leaves cut from green fruit roll-ups. There you have it! A flower that's good enough to eat!

Kelly W. Ricker, St. Francis Xavier School, Birmingham, AL

• Use this popular book to sprout interest in an upcoming plant unit. Challenge students (with the help of their parents) to collect a variety of seeds. Examine the resulting seed collections and find out who has the smallest (largest) seed. Then, using magnifiers, have students observe, compare, and describe the colors, sizes, and shapes of the seeds. If desired, have each student plant several seeds from his collection. Use the remaining seeds to create eye-catching mosaics.

Barbara D. O'Neal—Gr. 3, Hattiesburg, MS

A House For Hermit Crab

• Whenever a new student joins your class as a result of a move from another area, you have the perfect opportunity for reading *A House For Hermit Crab*. After reading the story, have students brainstorm ways to help new students adjust to their surroundings and develop lasting friendships.

Barbara D. O'Neal—Gr. 2, Hattiesburg, MS

• What better way to follow up this delightful book than to have each student illustrate the house of her dreams? After the students have completed their pictures, have them write paragraphs describing the details of their homes. After each student has shared her paragraph and illustration, compile the projects into a class booklet entitled "Dream Houses."

Andrea Masone—Gr. 2, Student Teacher, Spring Shadows Elementary, Houston, TX

• Not only is *A House For Hermit Crab* an excellent literature choice for a sea life unit; it also serves as a great sequencing activity. Give each of 12 student groups a length of bulletin-board paper labeled for a different month. Then—using only construction-paper scraps, glue, and scissors—have each group create a work of art on its paper that shows Hermit Crab's house during that month. After each group has shared its project, display the projects in sequence (according to the story) on a bulletin board entitled "A Year with Hermit Crab." Later use the project to create a student-made big book. To do this, remove the projects from the display, mount them on tagboard, and laminate them for durability. Bind the resulting booklet pages between a student-decorated poster-board entitled "A Year With Hermit Crab."

Karin Fisk—Gr. 1, Linda Vista School, Mission Viejo, CA

• The outcome of this project is well worth the time it takes students to create it. Each student needs a lunch bag and the following shapes duplicated on white construction paper: three shells in various sizes, a sea anemone, a starfish, a coral, a snail, a sea urchin, seaweed, a lanternfish, and a wall. Each student also needs two hermit crabs (one slightly larger than the other) duplicated on red construction paper. Using the story as a guide, have students cut out and decorate each of the story props in sequence. (If desired use a variety of art techniques to complete the props.) Have students store their completed story props in their lunch bags. When all of the props have been created, have students use them to retell the story. Arrange for interested students to visit other classrooms and share the story of Hermit Crab with small groups.

Sandy Greensfelder—Gr. 1, Naples Elementary, Naples, Italy

On Tuesday he ate through two skateboards. But he was still hungry.

The Very Hungry Caterpillar

• Once you've read *The Very Hungry Caterpillar*, have students recall the main events of the story. List these events on the chalkboard. Then give each student a number of paper plates that is one greater than the sum of the events listed on the board. Each student illustrates one event per paper plate; then he designs a caterpillar face on his remaining plate. To assemble a book, arrange the plates side by side in sequential order (positioning the caterpillar head at the front), slightly overlapping the plates' edges as shown. Then, using brads, fasten the plates together. When assembled properly, the book can be folded into a neat stack. Then as students enjoy their books, they can watch their caterpillars grow!

Christina Boyd—Librarian, Wilson Elementary, Collinsville, OK

• Bring the four stages of butterfly metamorphosis alive for your youngsters as they each make a representation of the cycle. To begin, visually divide a paper plate or a sheet of paper into fourths using a black marker. In one section, glue a construction-paper leaf. Then put a dried lentil atop a spot of glue to represent the butterfly *egg.* To represent the *larval stage,* twist three pipe-cleaner pieces together and glue wiggle eyes at one end. Glue this caterpillar to the second section. Or glue a series of pom-poms in this section to resemble a caterpillar. To represent the *pupal stage,* roll up a paper triangle and glue the resulting point in place, or roll up a small piece of cotton batting. Glue a small twig to the next section of the paper plate, and glue the rolled paper or batting to resemble a chrysalis. (Although some butterfly larvae spin cocoons around themselves, most develop a hard shell called a chrysalis.) To portray the *adult butterfly,* accordion-fold a tissue-paper square, secure it in a bent pipe-cleaner body, and spread the paper for the butterfly's wings. Glue the butterfly to the remaining paper-plate section.

• That caterpillar had the right idea when he filled up on fruit from Monday through Friday. In advance, collect and clean one styrofoam egg carton for every two students. Cut off each carton's lid; then cut each egg carton bottom in half so that two, six-section strips result. These strips will be caterpillar serving dishes. At the conclusion of the story, have students chop apples, pears, plums, strawberries, and oranges into bite-size pieces and display them in separate serving bowls. In another bowl, mix equal parts of fruit yogurt and Cool Whip. Also provide raisins, pretzels, and toothpicks. To serve, have each student spoon a few pieces of each fruit into a section of his caterpillar serving dish, spoon some yogurt mixture into the remaining section, and top it with raisin eyes and pretzel antennae. Hungry caterpillar lovers can then use toothpicks to dip each fruit piece in the yogurt mixture before gobbling down the tempting morsels.

• Using this idea, students author and illustrate slightly exaggerated adaptations of *The Very Hungry Caterpillar.* Duplicate a supply of open booklet pages like the one shown. Then, using one booklet page for each day of the week, a student describes what his caterpillar ate during a one-week period. Have students illustrate their booklet pages and organize them sequentially before stapling them between construction-paper covers.

Linda Patten—Gr. 3, Leary Elementary School, Honeoye Falls, NY
Elaine Kaplan—Grs. 1 & 2, Link School, New City, NY

The Grouchy Ladybug

• After reading *The Grouchy Ladybug,* use red poster board and black construction paper to create a giant-size booklet cover like the one shown. Using a stamp pad and a clock stamp, print a clock face on each of several booklet pages. Program one page for each hour of the school day. Then, on each page, write a class-generated description of the activities that normally take place during that hour. Next give each page to a small group of students to be illustrated. Finally sequence the completed pages and staple them inside the booklet cover. Older students will enjoy making personalized mini-versions of this timely booklet.

Elizabeth A. Main—Gr. 1, Davenport Elementary School, Davenport, FL

• No one will fly off angry when you ask him to supply a page for this class booklet. After each student has stamped an unprogrammed clock face onto a sheet of drawing paper, have him specify a time and program his clock accordingly. Next have each student copy, complete, and illustrate the following sentence: "At _____[time]_____ the ladybug met a _____." Punch matching holes in the left margin of each page and enlist the help of your youngsters in compiling the pages in sequential order. Use rings or yarn to bind the pages between a decorated cover.

Elaine Kaplan—Grs. 1 & 2, Link School, New City, NY

• *The Grouchy Ladybug* is an excellent addition to a unit on feelings. Make a class list of things that make your youngsters (and you!) grouchy. Next brainstorm a list of ways to overcome grouchiness. Then encourage students to refer to the lists as they write and illustrate stories in which the main characters become grouchy and then overcome their grouchy feelings.

Kelly McCalla—Gifted & Talented Teacher, Oakland School, Greenwood, SC

Papa, Please Get The Moon For Me

• Students may be moonstruck by this art project! After reading aloud the book, have each student sponge-paint a luncheon-size paper plate: first with gray paint, then with white. Allow the plates to dry while the students are finger-painting with blue finger paint on large sheets of paper. Have each student cut his plate to resemble a phase of the moon, glue it to his dried finger-painted paper, and attach some foil stars around the moon cutout. Oh, nice!

The Secret Birthday Message

• Your budding authors will be eager to create personalized versions of this unique birthday book. First have each student illustrate the perfect birthday gift on a sheet of drawing paper. Next have each student create a secret message that would lead him to the gift if he found the message under his pillow and the gift were hidden somewhere in his home. Then have students create the remaining pages of their books, encouraging them to cut some pages into different shapes just as Carle has done. Lastly, have the students sequence the pages of their stories and bind them between construction-paper covers.

Patty Cheek—Gr. 2, Camp Creek School, Lilburn, GA
Karin Fisk—Gr. 1, Linda Vista, Mission Viejo, CA

The Very Busy Spider

• Inspired by the very busy spider, your youngsters will delight in making their own webs. Give each student a thin, white paper plate. Have students create webs by arranging and gluing lengths of black yarn atop the plates in desired fashions. Or award the individual yarn lengths based on established criteria (such as reading a book, completing a homework assignment, or memorizing math facts), and have students build their webs over a series of days or weeks.

Julie Eick Granchelli, Warren P. Towne Elementary School, Medina NY

• After your youngsters have had the pleasure of hearing *The Very Busy Spider* and feeling her marvelous web, tempt their taste buds with spider snacks! Have each youngster spread cream cheese (tinted, if desired) between two round crackers, before inserting eight pretzel legs into the cheese. Youngsters complete the creepy-crawly effect by attaching two raisin eyes atop the cracker body using cream cheese.

• Have your youngsters decide on a new location for the very busy spider. Once a location (such as a zoo, circus, jungle, or desert) has been decided upon, have each youngster specify a creature found in that location. Then have him glue a tissue-paper representation of this creature on white art paper, along with a glue or glitter-and-glue web. Finally have him write a sentence including a sound the creature would make and a question for the spider. For example: "Hiss! Hiss!" said the snake. "Want to slither in the grass?" Join these pages with metal rings for lots of reading fun!

Eric Carle's Animals Animals

• In this commemorative volume, created especially for sharing, Carle has selected poetry and lyrical pieces from a myriad of sources and accompanied each piece with a brilliant full-color illustration. For a follow-up activity, have each student select an animal, create a tissue-paper collage of the animal, and then write an accompanying piece of poetry or prose. Compile the completed projects in a class booklet or display them on a bulletin board.

Cathy Conier—Gr. 1-4 LDR, Southeastern Elementary, Chesapeake, VA

Have You Seen My Cat?

• A boy's search for his lost pet leads him on such a wild cat chase that he's not sure he'll ever find it! But when he least expects it—there it is. Ask students what the boy could have done to make the search for his lost cat less of a wild cat chase, guiding them to the conclusion that a description of his cat would have been helpful. Then divide students into small groups. Have each group select a different cat from the story and write a description of it. Later have a student from each group read aloud the description he and his group members wrote. Challenge the remainder of the students to identify the lost cat.

Patty Cheek—Gr. 2, Camp Creek School, Lilburn, GA

Pancakes, Pancakes!

• Inspired by the story line of *Pancakes, Pancakes!,* your students can author and illustrate their own food-related stories. Have each student choose an edible item that requires preparation such as an apple pie or a strawberry shortcake. Next have each student list the ingredients that are needed to prepare this food item. Give each child a supply of story paper. Then, imitating the story line from the book, a child describes how his main character obtains each of the necessary ingredients. Encourage students to describe the steps on individual pages. Have students illustrate the pages of their stories before stapling each child's story between construction-paper covers. Move over, Eric Carle! There's a brood of young authors on the loose!

Julia Eick Granchelli, Warren P. Towne Elementary School, Medina, NY

• Just how do you make a pancake? For a fun follow-up activity, write your students' dictated version of a pancake recipe on a large pancake cutout. Next have students compare the recipe to an authentic pancake recipe. Conclude the activity with a cooking activity...pancakes, of course!

April Johnson—Gr. 1, Morningside Elementary, Perry, GA

• Creating a class graph of your youngsters' favorite pancake flavors is a perfect math extension to *Pancakes, Pancakes!* Brainstorm a list of pancake flavors such as blueberry, strawberry, chocolate chip, and plain. Then give each student a circular cutout. Have the students personalize and color the pancakes to reflect their favorite pancake flavors. Then have each student attach his pancake to a graph like the one shown.

Kathy Czarnecki—Gr. 1, Barrington Elementary, Florissant, MO

• Reinforce the importance of eating a healthful breakfast with this follow-up activity. Create a student-generated list of breakfast foods. Next have students evaluate the list and indicate which foods are nutritious and which are not. To complete the activity, divide students into groups and give each group a supply of discarded magazines. Then, working individually or as groups, have students create collages by gluing pictures of nutritious break-fast foods atop thin, white paper plates.

Kathy Czarnecki—Gr. 1

The Very Quiet Cricket

• This multisensory book is an excellent introduction to a unit on insects. The quiet cricket makes his way in the world, meeting one insect after another who greet the cricket with the cheery hellos of their species. But not until the end of the book is the cricket able to reply with a beautiful chirp that can be heard by your listeners as well. The book spans an entire day and each insect featured is presented during the time it is truly active. For example, the cricket meets a bumblebee during daylight hours and he meets a luna moth after the sun has gone down. Label a length of bulletin-board paper for each featured insect. Have students recall facts from the story and write these facts on the corresponding posters. Then challenge students to read and discover additional facts about these insects. Add the facts to the posters. Students can use the information on the posters to compare and contrast a bevy of bugs!

The Mixed-Up Chameleon

• These tissue-paper masterpieces can serve as bright reminders of *The Mixed-Up Chameleon.* Each student needs several different colors of tissue paper, glue, markers or crayons, a pencil, and a sheet of art paper. From each color of tissue paper, a student tears a body part from a different animal. He then assembles the pieces by gluing them to the art paper. Final touches such as facial features are added with crayons or markers. To complete the project, have each student write the name of his mixed-up critter and a sentence or two about it on his paper.

Lynn LaStrapes—Gr. 1, Wood River Elementary, Corpus Christi, TX

• Mixing and matching have never been more fun! For a fun follow-up project, divide students into groups and have each group cut out a variety of animal body parts (such as ears, tails, eyes and legs) from colorful construction paper. Next have each student in the group select several cutouts and glue them onto a sheet of white construction paper, creating an original mixed-up animal. When the projects are completed, invite each student to share his artwork with his classmates while giving a brief description of his animal's habitat and eating habits.

Jan Ross—Media Specialist, Dixie Elementary Magnet School Lexington, KY

• Find out what your youngsters would like to change about themselves with this journal-writing activity. In their journals have students describe what they would like to change about themselves, how these changes could be made, why they wish they could make these changes, and what effects these changes would have on their lives. Then, if desired, have students illustrate before and after self-portraits. Caution students to evaluate their wishes carefully—the chameleon learned a lesson for us all!

Barbara D. O'Neal—Gr. 3, Hattisburg, MS

A Timeline Of Titles

Culminate your study of Carle books with this timeline project. Write the title and publication date of each book presented on a large card; then give each card to a small group of students. Ask each group to illustrate the front of its card to represent the book title shown. On the back of the card, have each group write what it liked about the book. To create the timeline, secure both ends of a length of clothesline or heavy cord so that the line is taut. Then—in sequential order (based on the book's publication date)—have the groups present their completed cards, then clip them to the timeline using clothespins. The student-created display becomes a handy reference to Eric Carle books.

Patty Cheek—Gr. 2, Camp Creek School, Lilburn, GA

Bravo For Beverly Cleary!

Henry Huggins, Ramona Quimby, Ralph S. Mouse, and Muggie Maggie are just a few of Beverly Cleary's endearing storybook characters. Her books have become the favorites of many young readers, and in the classroom they rank as first-rate read-alouds. To complement your best-loved books from Cleary's outstanding collection, pick and choose from these classroom-tested suggestions.

Meet The Author

As a child growing up in Oregon amidst two world wars and economic hardships, Beverly Cleary longed to read honest stories of real kids and their true-life experiences. Later, as a children's librarian, Cleary found herself frustrated in her search for interesting, easy-to-read books that would speak to the average, ordinary child. Finally she decided to fill the void by writing her own children's books. Her first book, *Henry Huggins,* was published in 1950. To date Cleary has penned more than 30 books for young readers.

For a most delightful and accurate portrayal of Beverly Cleary as a child, a teenager, an adult, and a writer, read her autobiography *Beverly Cleary: A Girl From Yamhill* (William Morrow And Company, Inc.; 1988).

The Mouse And The Motorcycle

A mouse can't ride a motorcycle! But as Keith—the motorcycle's owner— soon discovers, this mouse isn't just any mouse!

Vroom! Vroom! Here's a creative-writing activity that's sure to get your students' wheels turning! Ask each child to pretend that he is the proud owner of a brand-new motorcycle. He may keep the bike for two weeks. Suggest that each child choose a travel destination and a riding partner (if desired), then write and illustrate a story about his motorcycle adventures. Vroooooooooooooom!

Jeannette M. Sweet
Newport Beach, CA

Trying to choose a favorite scene from *The Mouse And The Motorcycle* may be the most difficult part of this follow-up activity! Once students have made their selections, ask each child to re-create his favorite scene in the form of a diorama. Give each child a small empty box (a shoebox works well), and make available an assortment of construction paper and craft supplies such as fabric scraps, glitter, sequins, and pipe cleaners. Set aside small portions of time on each of several days for students to work on their projects. When the dioramas are complete, invite each youngster to present and explain the scene he depicted in his diorama.

Betty Kobes—Gr. 1
West Hancock Elementary
Kanawha, IA

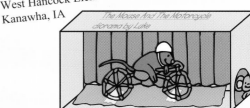

The Mouse And The Motorcycle diorama by Luke

Ramona Quimby, Age 8

There are trials and triumphs aplenty as Ramona Quimby, age 8, enters third grade.

When a hard-boiled egg fad begins at school, Ramona joins right in! But she's soon sorry that she did! After reading this portion of the story aloud, discuss the term *fad* with your youngsters. Ask students to brainstorm trends that are currently popular. Record their ideas on a chart labeled "What's Hot!"; then discuss how and why certain fads become popular and others do not. Follow up this discussion by challenging each student to design a poster that introduces a new fad. On a given date, encourage each child to share his fabulous new fad with his classmates!

Laura Lee Powers & Lisa Donahoo—Gr. 3
Bryant Elementary
Mableton, GA

For a lively discussion, ask students to talk about Ramona's relationship with her teacher, Mrs. Whaley. Find out how your students think Ramona rates as a student and how Mrs. Whaley rates as a teacher. For added fun, find out how your students think Ramona would adjust to a classroom taught by teachers featured in other books, such as Ms. Frizzle (Magic School Bus series), Viola Swamp or Miss Nelson *(Miss Nelson Is Missing!)*, or Mrs. Green *(The Teacher From The Black Lagoon)*. Conclude the discussion by having students write and illustrate want ads seeking the perfect teacher for Ramona.

Laura Lee Powers & Lisa Donahoo—Gr. 3

> ☆ Wanted ☆
> Nice, friendly teacher with lots of patience for an imaginative, high-spirited 8 year old!

After seeking advice from her father on how to "sell" her book to her class, Ramona decides to write her book report in the form of a television commercial. Your youngsters will enjoy selling their favorite books in the same way! Ask each youngster to create a poster that he feels will hook readers on his favorite book. Remind students that the name and author of the books they are selling must be featured on their posters. Display the resulting advertisements in a prominent location where passersby might also be "sold" on your youngsters' reading suggestions!

Tracy Hutcheson—Gr. 2, Featherstone Elementary
Woodbridge, VA

Don't be a Fruit Loop! Read Ramona by Beverly Cleary

Ramona can provide plenty of writing motivation for your youngsters! Her experiences are fun, yet so true-to-life that children easily relate to them. The following prompts are sure to get your youngsters writing!

- After reading about Ramona's first day of third grade, ask students to write about their most recent first-day-of-school experiences. You may find that your youngsters' impressions of their first day of school are somewhat different than you recall!
- Follow up chapter three by asking students to write about their most embarrassing moments.
- When Ramona and Beezus prepare Sunday dinner for their parents, it turns into quite an experience. Ask students to write about a time they tried to prepare a meal for their families. Or have students plan meals (with cooking instructions) that they would like to prepare for their families.
- At the conclusion of the book, the Quimbys are astounded by the kindness of an older gentleman. Ask the students to write about a time that an act of kindness took them by surprise, or about a time that they have surprised others with an act of kindness.

Barbara Rumsey
John Kennedy Elementary
Batavia, NY

Ramona And Her Father

When Mr. Quimby unexpectedly loses his job, Ramona takes an active hand in the challenges that develop.

Your students are sure to get down to business when you present them with this creative challenge! To begin ask students to recall Ramona's desire for a million dollars—an amount of money that was sure to solve all of her family's financial problems. Then challenge each student to create a make-believe business that she thinks would earn her a million dollars. Have each child design a 4" x 8" business card for her million-dollar business. Explain that each business card should include the name of the business, a catchy slogan that explains what the business produces or what service it provides, the student's name, and a business phone number. Then in turn have each entrepreneur display her business card as she explains her enterprise to her classmates.

Jennie Mehigan—Gr. 3
St. Hilary School
Akron, OH

When Ramona crafts a crown from burrs, she ends up in a very sticky situation. But when your youngsters create these crowns, they'll end up with one-of-a-kind headpieces and a better understanding of some real-life math skills. In advance set up a classroom store from which crown decorations (such as sequins, feathers, ribbon, lace, and imitation jewels) will be sold. To make a crown, a student draws, colors, and cuts out a construction-paper crown. He then takes a predetermined amount of play money to the store and buys the crown-making supplies he desires. (Each student should tally his purchases and determine the amount of change he is due.) Then he adorns his crown cutout with his purchases. Help each youngster secure his crown to the center of an 18" x 1 1/2" tagboard strip. Adjust the ends of the headband until the crown fits snugly on the child's head; then remove the crown and staple the head-band ends in place. There you have it! A crown like no other!

Peggy Wolke—Gr. 1
Graham North Elementary
Rosewood, OH

Ramona Forever

Ramona is back! And she has lots of surprises headed her way—a new job for her father, a wedding, and a new little Quimby!

What would be the perfect name for the newest Quimby? No doubt your youngsters will have an idea or two! On chart paper, record a student-generated list of names, sorting them into girl names and boy names. Narrow the list of names to the top five favorites in each category. Then, for added fun, ask student volunteers to find the meanings of the listed names in a book of baby names. Keep the class list of names posted until the name of the newest Quimby is revealed in the final chapter of the book.

Fran Rizzo—Gr. 3
Brookdale School
Bloomfield, NJ

Muggie Maggie

Maggie is far from thrilled about having to learn cursive writing. In fact, she decides she absolutely won't do it! Will Maggie ever change her mind?

Mrs. Leeper devises a plan! She writes cursive notes about Maggie; then she asks Maggie to deliver them to other teachers. Just as Mrs. Leeper had hoped, Maggie's curiosity gets the better of her and she peeks at the notes. Like Maggie, your youngsters are likely to be curious about the notes that you and other teachers write to one another. Build on that curiosity by asking each student to choose a teacher and write a note that he feels the selected teacher might write to a colleague. Increase the challenge by asking students to exchange and respond to each other's notes.

Kelli A. Thomas—Gr. 3
Otis Elementary School
Fremont, OH

> *Dear Ms. Thomas,*
> *You won't believe what happened! Jason's pet snake got loose this morning! The kids went wild. Remember play practice at 1:00.*
> *Mrs. Leeper*

Oops! Maggie didn't mean to spell her name "M-u-g-g-i-e." It was just her awful handwriting. But when her classmates see her mistake, they begin to call her "Muggie Maggie." If only she had written more carefully! Help your students learn the value of writing their own names carefully by having them purposely write their names carelessly. Ask each student to write various letters within her name incorrectly. For example, Sally might make her *a* look like an *i*. Then she would write her name as "Silly Sally." Plan to let students share their mistaken identities aloud.

Kaye Schilling—Gr. 3
Lake Cable Elementary
Canton, OH

To reinforce cursive skills, get students reading your cursive writing! Each morning write an intriguing question or comment on the chalkboard. Ask the students to read the sentence to themselves; then ask a volunteer to read the sentence aloud. If desired invite students to respond to the sentence in their journals. As students begin to improve their own cursive writing and reading abilities, leave cursive notes of praise on their desktops.

Pam Williams—Gr. 3
Dixieland Elementary
Lakeland, FL

> Wow! I can read this!

A Tour Of The Neighborhood

Through her wonderful stories, Cleary re-created her childhood neighborhood, moved it several blocks to Klickitat Street, and peopled it with lovable yet true-to-life characters. The result is a high-interest neighborhood that's perfect for reinforcing the concepts of neighborhood and community. Once your students are familiar with several of Cleary's books, have them work together to create a mural-size map of the neighborhood featured in Cleary's books. When the class project is complete, students can conduct neighborhood tours in which they share favorite events and humorous anecdotes about the neighborhood.

Patricia White—Librarian & Susan Gerritz—Gr. 3
Ventura Park Elementary School
Portland, OR

Happy Birthday, Tomie dePaola!

Since his childhood, Tomie dePaola has dreamt of touching the lives of others. DePaola once said, "It's a dream of mine that one of my books, any book, any picture, will touch the heart of some individual child and change that child's life for the better." DePaola has written and/or illustrated almost 200 books, including *The Art Lesson,* which is somewhat autobiographical. The selection of *Strega Nona* as a 1976 Caldecott Honor Book is among his numerous awards and honors. The critically acclaimed success and continued popularity of his books make it apparent that dePaola is indeed realizing his dream.

Tomie dePaola's birthday is on September 15. If your youngsters develop a special fondness for dePaola's books, consider having them make a group birthday card and mailing it to the author in care of The Putnam & Grosset Group, 200 Madison Avenue, New York, NY 10016. Happy birthday, Mr. dePaola!

From STREGA NONA MEETS HER MATCH by Tomie dePaola. Copyright©1993 by Tomie dePaola. Used by permission of G. P. Putnam's Sons, a division of Penguin Putnam Inc.

The Art Lesson
Published by G. P. Putnam's Sons

Although you can never be certain just how many dePaolas are in your class, you can be fairly confident that this story will strike an inspiring chord with many of your little ones. Before reading *The Art Lesson* aloud, explain to your students that the author and the book character have several things in common, such as: a dad who was a barber, Irish grandparents, an Italian grandmother, an art teacher named Beulah Bowers, and the desire to be a REAL artist. Then read the story while wearing an apron that has one or more pockets which have been filled with elements from the story. Some of the things you may want to tuck into the apron pockets include: a comb (representing Tommy's dad's barber shop), a fruit (representing his grandparents' grocery store), a flashlight (like the one Tommy used under the sheets), large chalks (like the ones the art teacher had), a box of 64 crayons (like the one Tommy received for his birthday), and a box of eight crayons (like the school crayons). As you are reading the story aloud, pull each prop from the apron at the appropriate moment to bring the story alive. Later, ask each child to design a special award for himself as a tribute to his particular talents or skills.

Kelly Pflederer—Gr. 2
Academy Of The Sacred Heart, St. Charles, MO

Even when he was a kindergartner, Tommy knew that he wanted to be a REAL artist when he grew up. And he knew that REAL artists don't copy! As your students will see when you've finished a reading of *The Art Lesson,* Tommy *did* grow up to be a real artist. Have students think about what they would really like to be when they grow up. Encourage each student to write about these dreams. When it's time to send these papers home, accompany them with a description of the story and the assignment that the youngsters completed. In the note, encourage each parent to put the paper away with other mementos. After many years have passed, parents can enjoy rereading their children's ambitions and seeing how they relate to their current talents.

Deb Marciano Boehm—Gr. 2, Woodridge School, Cranston, RI

Tom
Published by G. P. Putnam's Sons

In his newest autobiographical picture book, dePaola champions the special relationship he had with his grandfather, after whom he is named. Youngsters will enjoy the mischievous bond between grandfather and grandson. This story is a treasure!

Strega Nona

Published by Simon And Schuster
Books For Young Readers

This follow-up activity for dePaola's Caldecott Honor Book, *Strega Nona,* is a great tie-in with your letter-writing unit. Read aloud *Strega Nona;* then ask each of your youngsters to imagine that he is one of the townspeople from the story. Have him decorate the blank side of a lined 5" x 8" index card to resemble a postcard showing a town landmark. On the other side of the card, have him write a fictitious address for Strega Nona at a friend's house, along with a plea for Strega Nona to hurry home to help with the mess that Big Anthony made. If desired, bind the student-made postcards into a booklet titled "Come Quick, Strega Nona!" for students' enjoyment.

Cheryl Sergi—Gr. 2, Greene Central School, Greene, NY

Strega Nona will be an instant hit with your youngsters, but so will these follow-up activities. After reading the story to your students, give each student a helping of long, chilled spaghetti seasoned with a touch of Italian salad dressing. In turn, have each student pose for a photograph that will show his favorite spaghetti-eating technique. Some students may neatly down their carefully twirled forkfuls of spaghetti, while others may exhibit unusual eating styles such as spaghetti "slurping." On a bulletin board, display the developed pictures along with student-made pasta art. Heighten the element of fun by unveiling this display on a day when spaghetti will be served for lunch.

Christina Boyd—Librarian K-3
Wilson Elementary, Collinsville, OK

Readers are led to believe that Strega Nona has very unorthodox methods for making pasta. Ask youngsters to think about how someone makes spaghetti. Have each student write the process in his own words. Then have each student copy the directions—one per strip—onto narrow strips of manila paper, and write his name on the back of each strip. To store the strips, have each student glue the edges—but not the top—of a black pot cutout to a sheet of paper. Instruct students to slide the spaghetti-making direction strips into their pots for storage. Encourage students to take turns sequencing the strips of their classmates.

Lisa Vanderburg—Grs. 3 and 4, Everett Elementary, Paris, TX

Strega Nona's
Pasta Pot
Big Anthony, Keep Out!

From STREGA NONA MEETS HER MATCH by Tomie dePaola. Copyright©1993 by Tomie dePaola. Used by permission of G. P. Putnam's Sons, a division of Penguin Putnam Inc.

Strega Nona's Magic Lessons

Published by Harcourt Brace, Publishers

In this book, Strega Nona is teaching her magic secrets to two young girls—one of whom is actually Big Anthony in disguise. Read aloud *Strega Nona's Magic Lessons;* then use the story as the basis of ongoing integrated lessons. Begin by having students decorate large cardboard cutouts to resemble Strega Nona's house. At first, have students use the cutouts as the backdrop for a reenactment of the story. Then use the cutouts as room dividers to perpetuate the Strega Nona theme. Later have each student cut a pot shape from black tagboard or poster board. Working in cooperative groups, have the students look through copies of *Strega Nona's Magic Lessons* in search of nouns. Make a cumulative list of all the nouns identified; then have each child select a few nouns to write on oval "pasta" cutouts and suspend on thread beneath his pot cutout. On another day, have students search for verbs or adjectives to add beneath their pots. Soon there'll be pasta everywhere!

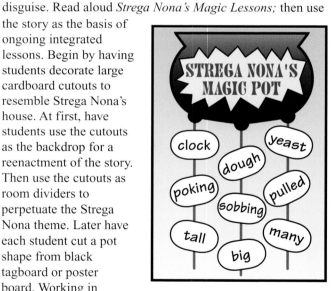

STREGA NONA'S MAGIC POT

clock   yeast   dough   poking   pulled   sobbing   tall   big   many

Sandy Greensfelder—Gr. 1
Naples Elementary, Naples, Italy

Strega Nona Meets Her Match

Published by G. P. Putnam's Sons

In her latest adventure, it looks as if old-fashioned Strega Nona is going to be upstaged by a modern-thinking healer. When Strega Amelia comes to town, she brings more than gossip. Soon she has set up her own shop and is using the latest modern gadgets to treat Strega Nona's regular customers! It looks like Strega Nona's met her match, unless she has her own *cure* for Strega Amelia!

Big Anthony's Mixed-Up Magic

A CD-ROM adventure from Putnam New Media

Once your students are thoroughly hooked on the Strega Nona books, they'll go hook, line, and sinker for *Big Anthony's Mixed-Up Magic.* In this CD-ROM adventure, youngsters can visit Strega Nona's medieval world. Once there, they can read and hear and watch the story, help Big Anthony as he bumbles through his jobs, try magic tricks, and play a music-writing game. Ask your librarian to locate this CD-ROM program for you, or call The Putnam Publishing Group at 1-800-631-8571 for ordering information.

From STREGA NONA MEETS HER MATCH by Tomie dePaola. Copyright©1993 by Tomie dePaola. Used by permission of G. P. Putnam's Sons, a division of Penguin Putnam Inc.

The Popcorn Book

Published by Holiday House

Put the "Yum!" into a reading of *The Popcorn Book* with this suggestion. In advance, prepare for this story by bagging some popcorn for each child. Then, before you begin reading, ask students to only eat a kernel of popcorn each time the word *popcorn* is mentioned in the book. Since the word *popcorn* occurs repeatedly in the story, youngsters can enjoy a great healthful snack while you read. When the totally yummy story is done, permit students to munch out on any remaining popcorn leftovers.

Leigh Anne Newsom—Gr. 3
Greenbrier Intermediate School, Chesapeake, VA

From STREGA NONA MEETS HER MATCH by Tomie dePaola. Copyright©1993 by Tomie dePaola. Used by permission of G. P. Putnam's Sons, a division of Penguin Putnam Inc.

There's lots to learn—including history and science—between these covers. So read *The Popcorn Book* aloud; then make popcorn using a recipe from the book. Have students measure the amount of unpopped popcorn used to prepare the recipe. Then have them measure the popped corn and compare the two measures. Since such a delicious atmosphere has been set, have students write popcorn-related poetry or make a contribution to a class big book while they munch and crunch. Or have them string the excess popped corn to make jewelry. For a social studies tie-in, have students use a globe or maps to locate each of the geographic areas mentioned in the book.

Jane Ursida, Ozone Park, NY

THE POPCORN BOOK by Class 2J

Fin M'Coul: The Giant Of Knockmany Hill

Published by Holiday House

Fin M'Coul's work on the Giant's Causeway (a true natural wonder in Northern Ireland) is interrupted by the nasty giant Cucullin. But Fin's lovely wife Oonagh soon comes to the rescue. Read the story aloud, stopping before Oonagh's plan is revealed. Have your youngsters brainstorm how Oonagh could help her husband. Explain that this is a fairy tale, so no idea is too farfetched to be woven into the story. Ask for volunteers to continue the story. Once students have given several possible endings, read the remainder of the book. Find out which ending is the favorite of your youngsters.

Deb Marciano Boehm—Gr. 2, Woodridge School, Cranston, RI

In *Fin M'Coul: The Giant Of Knockmany Hill,* Oonagh works a charm by braiding thread into a bracelet, an anklet, and a circle pin. Students thoroughly enjoy her clever plot to undo the mean-spirited Cucullin. After reading the story to youngsters, have each student make a bracelet similar to the one Oonagh made. To make a bracelet, knot together three different-colored strands of embroidery floss. Tape the knotted end to a tabletop. Braid the three strands of floss together; then knot the loose end. Remove the tape. Wrap the braided embroidery floss around a wrist and tie it in place. Wouldn't it be nice  if this bracelet assured that the wearer could not fail at what he attempted. Find out what your youngsters would choose to do, if they knew they could not fail.

Patricia McClune—Librarian K-6
Brownstown Elementary, Brownstown, PA

The Mysterious Giant Of Barletta

Published by Harcourt Brace Jovanovich, Publishers

A little old Italian woman and a giant's statue pair up to defend the town of Barletta from the army of an enemy. Zia Concetta, the woman, divulges the plan only to the statue. The rest of the locals hide from the approaching army. After having students locate Italy on a map, read *The Mysterious Giant Of Barletta,* stopping before Zia's plan is revealed. Have students think of ways that the old lady and a statue of a giant could defeat an entire army. Then continue reading the story. Afterward, talk about different kinds of onions. Be sure to mention that one kind of onion is actually named the Barletta onion. If desired, have students bring in onions for making French onion soup in a Crock-Pot.

Deb Marciano Boehm—Gr. 2

Little Grunt And The Big Egg: A Prehistoric Fairy Tale

Published by Holiday House

Making a few unusual preparations before you share this story with your students can lead to BIG fun when the story's done. In advance, use tempera to paint an egg-shaped watermelon to resemble a dinosaur egg. Hide it somewhere on the school grounds. Read *Little Grunt And The Big Egg* to your students; then explain that something that resembles a dinosaur egg has been spotted at school. Ask students to write speculative stories about the appearance of the egg and what it contains. Then have students search until they find the imitation dinosaur egg. When all the hubbub about the dinosaur egg has begun to fade away, serve the watermelon to the students for a snack.

Kelly McCaller—Gifted And Talented
Oakland School, Greenwood, SC

Pancakes For Breakfast

Published by Harcourt Brace Jovanovich

Today's youngsters—accustomed to supermarket and fast-food fare—may be surprised to realize just how hard it can be to round up the ingredients for pancakes. When "reading" this story with your youngsters, pause when the lady is on the way back with the syrup, and ask youngsters what will happen next. Turn the page and have students comment on the destruction by the pets and the lady's chances of having pancakes this particular morning. Then finish the story. Using the book's recipe, have students prepare pancakes. While they're feasting on these flapjacks, have youngsters contrast their pancake-making experience to that of the lady in the story.

Quite A Character!

If your students are studying the works of Tomie dePaola, they'll have a great time selecting and describing a dePaola character for this activity. After students are familiar with several of dePaola's books, ask each student to select his favorite character. Then provide him with a shield cutout that has been visually divided into several sections. In each section, have the student write something different about the character. For example, one section might be used to record special talents of the character, another might be used to tell about the character's occupation, and yet another might be used to tell how the character probably feels in a particular story. If desired, encourage each student to decorate his shield with designs that are befitting of the character. When each student has completed a shield, have him read the information on his shield to his classmates without divulging the name of the character. Find out how many of your students recognize the character from the student's descriptions.

Lisa Vanderburg—Grs. 3 and 4
Everett Elementary, Paris, TX

How Do They Compare?

Once your youngsters are familiar with several of Tomie dePaola's books, they can use Venn diagrams to compare and contrast his books. Ask students to choose two books at a time to compare. For example, you could begin by comparing *Nana Upstairs & Nana Downstairs* and *Now One Foot, Now The Other.* First read both stories. Then draw a Venn diagram on the board and have students name elements that are shared by the stories and elements that are unique to each story. Have students examine several of dePaola's books in this manner. Are there more similarities than they might have first believed, or more differences?

Lisa Vanderburg—Grs. 3 and 4

From STREGA NONA MEETS HER MATCH by Tomie dePaola. Copyright©1993 by Tomie dePaola.
Used by permission of G. P. Putnam's Sons, a division of Penguin Putnam Inc.

From STREGA NONA MEETS HER MATCH by Tomie dePaola. Copyright©1993 by Tomie dePaola.
Used by permission of G. P. Putnam's Sons, a division of Penguin Putnam Inc.

Dimensional Display

Strega Nona, one of Tomie dePaola's most popular characters, was known to have a pasta pot that overflowed. If your display areas are overflowing with dePaola-related projects, consider this alternative display. Have each student bring to school a square or nearly square lidded box, or provide a box for each student. Instruct students to cover their boxes with colorful paper. Then have them attach some of their projects onto the sides of the boxes. The character shields described in "Quite A Character!", the Venn diagrams described in "How Do They Compare?", and the pasta-filled pots described in the third paragraph under *Strega Nona* (page 20) are examples of projects that would look great on the sides of these boxes. Stack the boxes for a three-dimensional display that all your students can take pride in.

Lisa Vanderburg—Grs. 3 and 4

Activities To Use With

Lois Ehlert's Books

Collage is Lois Ehlert's favorite art technique. To make a collage, an artist cuts out pieces of paper or fabric and glues them to a backing. Lois Ehlert has been cutting and gluing for as long as she can remember. And as far back as she can recall, her parents were creating things. Her dad did some woodworking in a basement workshop, and her mother did a lot of sewing. To Lois's delight her parents set up a card table to be her very own working area. Long before Lois Ehlert became a renowned artist/author, she sat at that card table and used scrap lumber and nails donated by her father and fabric scraps contributed by her mother to create her earliest works of art.

Use your choice of books by Lois Ehlert with the activities suggested, and you'll find that her books help you to unveil fascinating information, create a sense of wonder, and unlock the creativity within your youngsters.

ideas contributed by Lenell Lindsey—Gr. 2, Len Lastinger Elementary, Tifton, GA

Get To Know Lois Ehlert

Published by Harcourt Brace & Company

One good way for students to get to know Lois Ehlert and her work is by watching the video *Get To Know Lois Ehlert.* By watching this 20-minute videotape, students can learn about Lois's childhood and things in her life that have inspired her books. They can also see how Lois starts with a model, such as her sister's cat or fresh fruit from the market, and creates a work of art that bears a striking resemblance to the model. The videotape, which retails for $40.00, may be ordered from your local bookstore or by calling Harcourt Brace customer service at 1-800-543-1918.

Fish Eyes: A Book You Can Count On

Published by Harcourt Brace Jovanovich

Although Lois Ehlert is a nonswimmer, it was her musings about what it would be like to swim with fish that compelled her to write and illustrate *Fish Eyes: A Book You Can Count On.* Prepare for this activity by obtaining different colors of neon paper and large sheets of dark-blue construction paper; then read the story aloud to your students. After discussing the book with your students, have them collectively select one fish from the book to describe. As the students suggest words that describe the fish, note the words on the board. Then encourage each student to cut the neon papers and glue them to a sheet of construction paper to create a unique fish. When each student has finished his fish artwork, have him write (or dictate for you to write) several words that describe the fish. Then have him mount the paper bearing the description of the fish on the construction paper with the fish artwork. Compile these projects in a student-made booklet or use them to make an attractive bulletin-board display.

Ask your students to take another look at *Fish Eyes: A Book You Can Count On* in an effort to find a word hidden in the scales of a fish. If it's necessary to narrow the search, hint that students should investigate the book's first two-page spread.

spotted
scaled
chubby
bright

glowing
orange

Red Leaf, Yellow Leaf

Published by Harcourt Brace Jovanovich

Lois Ehlert has planted many trees with her family. But in this story, she chronicles the life of a favorite sugar maple that has been around much longer than she has. Read *Red Leaf, Yellow Leaf* aloud to your youngsters. Then visit a nursery or invite a tree specialist to talk to your students about how to plant and care for a tree. If your students have any questions about things that are mentioned in the book, ask the expert to address them. Later, if possible, have your students help you plant a tree where it can easily be monitored. If planting a tree is not feasible, have your students adopt one already growing on school property. As the school year passes, have youngsters fill a scrapbook with tree trivia, photos, pressed leaves, seeds, flowers, and observations related to the seasonal changes and general growth of their tree. On Arbor Day in the spring, gather your students around their tree and review the entries in the scrapbook to reminisce about how the tree has changed since it was planted or adopted.

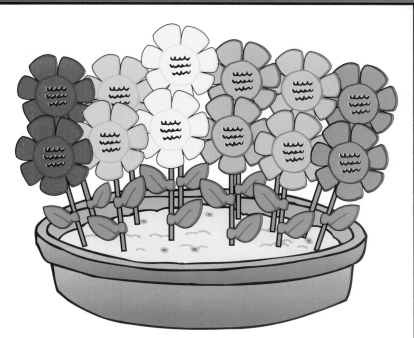

Circus

Published by HarperCollins

There's a Great Circus Parade every year in Milwaukee, Wisconsin. Inspired by the antique circus wagons in the parade, Milwaukee resident Lois Ehlert wrote *Circus*. Prepare to read this story to your students by reading the story privately and locating some circus music, if desired. Then, when you read the story aloud to students, use lots of expression to add to the drama. Afterward have students brainstorm elements from the story for which they could create sound effects. Have students audition for the part of the ringmaster, while other students work in groups to perfect assigned sound effects. Practice with the remainder of the students so that they will applaud, cheer, "ooohhh," and "aaahhh" on cue. Record the students' joint efforts as they retell the story with sound effects and circus music. Then place the recording in a center with a copy of *Circus* and headphones, and encourage students to silently read the book while listening to the tape.

Planting A Rainbow

Published by Harcourt Brace Jovanovich

If any of your youngsters have helped adults plant flowers, they'll especially love this story about flower gardening. Read *Planting A Rainbow* aloud. Then ask youngsters if they have planted or tended flowers. Ask volunteers who have already had flower-gardening experience to tell about their experiences. From those students who haven't yet become flower gardeners, find out what kinds of flowers they would like to grow and tend. Have each student make a contribution to a classroom rainbow of flowers with the following project.

To make a flower, paint a lightweight paper plate (front and back) using your choice of red, orange, yellow, green, blue, or purple tempera paint. When the paint has dried, scallop or fringe the plate to resemble the petals of a giant flower. On a five-inch paper circle, write something about your previous experiences with flower gardening or future gardening experiences you would like to have. Attach the construction-paper circle to the plate flower to represent the flower's center. To the back of the flower, attach a dowel rod which has been painted green. Attach leaf cutouts to the dowel, before "planting" this and other flowers in an oversize planter or pot filled with sand or fitted with a large piece of Styrofoam®.

Nuts To You!

Published by Harcourt Brace Jovanovich

After Lois Ehlert had to get a squirrel out of her apartment one day, she decided that a squirrel story was definitely in order. That's how *Nuts To You!* came to be. Read the story aloud to your youngsters. Discuss the squirrels they have seen at home and at school. Also ask each student to imagine that a squirrel paid him a visit in his house. Find out what mischief the squirrel might get into in each child's house.

Encourage each student to use the following process to make a peek-through illustration featuring a pesky squirrel: Begin by making several crayon rubbings of the bark of trees. If desired, brush a wash of watercolor over the rubbings. When the paint is dry, cut or tear the rubbings into strips. Then use water-thinned glue to attach the strips to a large sheet of art paper to resemble tree bark. Fold the art paper in half when it has dried. Trace a circular object onto the folded paper and cut out the resulting circle (cutting through only one paper layer), to create a hole similar to that on the cover of Lois Ehlert's book. Unfold the paper. On the blank side of the paper, glue paper cutouts to create a scene showing a squirrel making mischief inside a house. Position the squirrel art so that when the paper is refolded, the squirrel's face can be seen through the circular opening. If desired, refold the paper and use a marker to write, "Here's a squirrel from a tree. Wouldn't he rather play with me?" on the outside. Unfold the paper and write (inside) something about what the squirrel is doing in the illustration. To incorporate each student's artwork into a booklet, stack and bind the folded projects between poster-board covers.

Eating The Alphabet: Fruits And Vegetables From A To Z

Published by Harcourt Brace Jovanovich

To illustrate *Eating The Alphabet,* Lois Ehlert went to the market and gathered—a few at a time—the fruits and vegetables that she intended to illustrate. She brought them home and illustrated them one-by-one. After reading *Eating The Alphabet* aloud to your youngsters and discussing the foods shown, find out how many of your youngsters have tried each of the foods. Make an extended graph (or several separate smaller graphs) that bears a fruit or vegetable name for each letter of the alphabet. Using a miniature stamp and a stamp pad, have each student indicate the foods that he has tried by stamping a design in each of the appropriate columns. When every student has contributed to the graph, have the students analyze and summarize the results. Enlist the help of students in gathering and serving several of the least-tried foods.

A	B	C	D	E	F	G	H	I	J	K	L
		●				●			●		
	●	●				●			●	●	
●	●	●	●	●	●	●			●	●	
apricot	beet	cauliflower	date	eggplant	fig	grapes	huckleberry	Indian corn	jalapeño	kiwifruit	leek

Moon Rope

Published by Harcourt Brace Jovanovich

In this Peruvian tale, adapted by Lois Ehlert, a fox is consumed with the desire to go to the moon. The fox sets his goal and reaches the moon, but his friend the mole loses sight of the goal and settles for a lifetime underground. Ask each student to decide what he would want, if he could have anything. Then have him make the moon-rope project described below.

To make a moon rope, cut a paper plate into a crescent shape to resemble a crescent moon. Write the chosen goal on the moon cutout. Then, on three different crepe-paper streamers, write specific things that can be done to reach this goal. Tape the streamers together at one end. Then braid them, and secure the loose end to a personalized star with tape. Attach the other end of the braided streamers to the moon cutout, before suspending the project from the ceiling.

Mole's Hill:
A Woodland Tale

Published by Harcourt Brace & Company

Native American art forms inspired the artwork for Lois Ehlert's new book, *Mole's Hill.* In the story, a mole is asked by other woodland animals to move her unsightly little dirt mound. But the little mole loves her home so much that she develops an ingenious plan to change the perspectives of her neighbors. By the story's end, her neighbors insist that the mound not be disrupted.

Challenge your students to use their imaginations and creativity to turn rather unsightly things into works of art. Enlist the help of your students in collecting old pieces of junk that have little appeal. Things like old boots, empty unbreakable containers, old magazines, paper grocery bags, old silk flowers, scraps of fabric, and sewing notions are just a few of the things to start with. Also provide any art supplies needed by the students. Then have students—working individually, in pairs, or in small groups—use the available materials to create works of art. When the projects are complete, set up a classroom gallery containing students' projects and articles about other artists who start with rather unsightly things and convert them into works of art. Invite neighboring classes to view the exhibition.

Feathers For Lunch

Published by Harcourt Brace Jovanovich

Students may be interested to know that Lois Ehlert's sister's cat was the model for the cat in this book. After reading aloud *Feathers For Lunch,* ask students to describe how the cat probably felt as he was being carried back inside. Then encourage students to imagine that they could open a restaurant just for cats. Have the students work in small groups to design menus for a restaurant called Cat Cafe. Provide a folded sheet of tagboard and art supplies for each group, so that the students can note the menu items and design artwork in keeping with the Cat Cafe theme. When the work is complete, have each group show its menu and tell the advantages of dining at their Cat Cafe over capturing birds in the wild.

Growing Vegetable Soup

Published by Harcourt Brace Jovanovich

As a child, Lois Ehlert loved to garden with her parents. Now she's passing along that pleasure to a whole new generation of potential gardeners. After reading the story aloud to your youngsters, ask each child to bring a specified amount of an ingredient for the vegetable soup recipe (on the book jacket) on a specified day. Ask each student to attempt to locate an old hat to be converted into a work of garden art. (Pick up a few extra hats at a discount store or a store that resells used clothing.) Also ask students to collect small, free or inexpensive things related to gardening. Seed packets, descriptive plant stakes, plastic trowels, old gardening gloves, toy watering cans, vines, raffia, and silk or dried flowers are some things youngsters may be able to collect in preparation for making garden hats. If desired, have each student take another look at *Growing Vegetable Soup* before choosing a vegetable or vegetables to fashion out of papier-mâché. When the papier-mâché vegetables have been painted, assist students in using pipe cleaners to attach their garden-related items to their hats in creative manners. Time the completion of the hats so that they will be finished on the day that you'll be making soup. Invite each student to help make the soup, and when it's time to eat, remind them to wear their garden-art hats. Afterward, display the hats in a showcase for everyone to enjoy.

There's Just No Match For Mem!

Mem Fox is one of Australia's most popular children's book authors. She was born in Melbourne, Australia, on March 5, 1946. When she was only six months old she moved with her parents, who were both missionaries, to Africa. It was there—at a mission called Hope Fountain—that Mem grew up climbing trees, riding bikes, reading, and writing. Mem was only ten years old when she proudly presented her mother with an oral reading of her first book. To this day, Fox fondly remembers how her mother struggled to stay awake as she expounded on the subject of soil erosion!

In the mid-60s, Mem left Africa to attend drama school in London. There she met and married Malcolm Fox, and together they returned to Australia in 1970. Eight years later Mem Fox wrote her first book—*Possum Magic.* Her manuscript was rejected for publication nine different times over the next five years. Exasperated, Fox buried the manuscript in a desk drawer. If it hadn't been for Fox's husband, it might still be there today! Fortunately he convinced Fox to resubmit the manuscript, and this time it was accepted. Now an internationally published book, *Possum Magic* has won several awards and is the best-selling children's book in the history of Australia.

Mem Fox currently resides in South Australia. In addition to being a world-famous author, she is a senior lecturer in education at Flinders University in Adelaide, South Australia. She also travels around the world to speak at schools and conferences.

Use these classroom-tested suggestions to complement your favorite Mem Fox books.

Possum Magic
Illustrated by Julie Vivas
Harcourt Brace Jovanovich, Publishers; 1983

Possum Magic is Mem Fox's first picture book. The book is dedicated to Chloë, Fox's only child. Fox's inspiration for writing the book came from her realization that there were very few books about Australia that could be read by or to young Australians.

What could be more fun than touring the island continent of Australia with two adorable possums? In the story, Grandma and Hush Poss search for the perfect people food to reverse a seemingly innocent bit of magic that Grandma has performed. Their search takes them on a fascinating culinary tour of several Australian cities. Using pushpins or sticky dots, have youngsters chart the possums' journey on a wall map as you read the story aloud a second time. As each city is marked on the map, refer to the glossary at the back of the book to read the descriptions of the foods that were eaten there. After each description, take a poll to determine how popular the cuisine would be with your students.

Extend your exploration of Australia with this mapping project. After students have familiarized themselves with the travels of Grandma and Hush, challenge them to further explore the continent of Australia. To do this, divide students into eight small groups. Assign each group a different Australian state or territory to research. If desired, give each group a precut, poster-board cutout of its state or territory that can later be joined together with the other groups' cutouts to form a complete map of Australia. Ask each group to label its cutout with the names of the cities, geographical features, and wildlife that can be found there.

Stacey Leitzel—Gr. 2, New Market, VA

Wilfrid Gordon McDonald Partridge

Illustrated by Julie Vivas
Kane/Miller Book Publishers, 1985

This is Mem Fox's second picture book; however, it was the first of her books to be published in the United States. The idea for the story sprang from an incident when Fox was forewarning her daughter that she was about to lose her temper. Later Fox pondered why things like tempers and memories are always lost, but never found. In the book, a young boy with a very long name helps his elderly friend, Miss Nancy, find her memory. Why the name Wilfrid Gordon McDonald Partridge, one might ask? It's the full name of Mem Fox's father.

After a bit of research, Wilfrid Gordon develops a plan. To help Miss Nancy find her memory, he must take her something warm, something from long ago, something that made him cry, something that made him laugh, and something as precious as gold. Have your students consider what special gifts, fitting into these categories, they would bring to Miss Nancy. Then ask each student to bring his gift items to school for the day. Plan time for each child to share his collection of items and the memory associated with each one.

Leigh Anne Newsom—Gr. 3
Greenbrier Intermediate
Chesapeake, VA

It makes no difference if you're young, old, or in between—memories are made every day. Ask students to think about their special memories, and discuss how these memories could be preserved. Lead students to conclude that one of the most magical things about writing is how it can help people hold onto their memories. Then present each child with a personalized journal. Encourage students to write about their memories in these special journals. Writing in your own memory journal will serve as added inspiration for your young writers.

Tami Seal—Gr. 1, Widen Elementary
Austin, TX

Encourage your students to develop friendships with the elderly by planning a trip to a local senior citizen facility. Make arrangements for youngsters to spend time visiting with the residents. During your visit, find out if the residents there might be interested in developing pen-pal relationships with your students. Explore all options, from individual pen pals to having one resident reply to an occasional class letter.

Marnie Cole—Grs. 2 & 3
Village Elementary School, Syosset, NY

Koala Lou

Illustrated by Pamela Lofts
Harcourt Brace Jovanovich, Publishers; 1988

In Koala Lou, a soft and round koala comes up with a plan to recapture the attention of her once doting mother. In the end, Koala Lou realizes she didn't need a plan at all. Mem Fox admits that this story is about her relationship with her mother—a woman who showed her love in many ways, but not by saying the three words Mem longed to hear the most.

When Koala Lou places second in the Bush Olympics, she hides in a tree and cries her heart out. Tell about a time that you experienced disappointment as a child, and invite your students to do the same. Ask students how they deal with their disappointments. Do they prefer to talk about what has happened with someone? And if so, whom? Or do they prefer to spend time alone in a special place? Ask students to write about their most recent disappointments and explain how they overcame, or are working on overcoming, these feelings. Have students illustrate their completed stories.

Marsha Portnoy—Reading Teacher, Village Elementary School, Syosset, NY

Night Noises

Illustrated by Terry Denton
Harcourt Brace Jovanovich, Publishers; 1989

Mem Fox is up to a few tricks in this delightfully suspenseful story that youngsters will enjoy hearing again and again. Lily Laceby is nearly 90 years old and lives in a remote cottage with her dog, Butch Aggie. One wild winter night, she drifts off to sleep. As she dreams peacefully of days gone by, Butch hears a series of strange noises. Who could be out on such a cold winter night?

These doggie diaries will have your students ready to write—no bones about it! To make the diaries, duplicate two construction-paper copies of the bone pattern on page 52 for each student. Have each child cut out her bone shapes, then use one cutout as a template to trace and cut out a desired number of blank writing pages. Next the student staples the blank pages between the two covers and decorates her journal as desired. Then, writing from Butch Aggie's point of view, have each youngster describe the night of Lily Laceby's 90th birthday. Suggest that students include illustrations that show what Butch might have been thinking as she barked and carried on in response to the different noises that she heard. Before any writing begins, study the illustrations in *Night Noises* with your students. No doubt they'll discover that Butch Aggie is quite a pooch!

Cheryl Gardner—Gr. 2, Brownell Talbot School, Omaha, NE

This story beckons to have a sound track that includes lots of scary noises! Enlist the help of your youngsters in creating sounds for the different noises heard by Butch. Then read the story aloud several times in a row, and have students make the agreed-upon sounds at the appropriate points in the story. Next record the production on a cassette tape. Finally plan a birthday bash in honor of Lily Laceby's 90th birthday. Have students design and deliver party invitations to their parents. Plan to play the sound track during the party and serve birthday cake. Lily would probably like to have a few birthday games played in her honor, too!

Vicki Giermann—Grs. K–1 Multiage, Laveen School, Laveen, AZ

More Books By Mem Fox

Tough Boris
Illustrated by Kathryn Brown
Harcourt Brace & Company, 1994

Here is a rollicking adventure about Boris van der Borch—a mean, greedy old pirate who's tough as nails. Or is he? When a young boy sneaks onto Boris's ship, he discovers that the pirates on board aren't quite what he had expected.

Sophie
Illustrated by Aminah Brenda Lynn Robinson
Harcourt Brace & Company, 1994

Written in memory of her grandfather, Mem Fox describes the love shared between a young girl and her grandfather.

Shoes From Grandpa
Illustrated by Patricia Mullins
Orchard Books, 1989

In this cumulative rhyme, Grandpa buys a new pair of shoes for Jessie. Then several family members describe the clothing they plan to buy for Jessie to go with her new shoes. In the end Jessie lets it be known that what she really wants is a new pair of jeans.

Time For Bed
Illustrated by Jane Dyer
Harcourt Brace & Company, 1993

The rhythmic verse and tender watercolor illustrations make this book a perfect choice for lulling young children to sleep.

Hattie And The Fox
Illustrated by Patricia Mullins
Bradbury Press, 1987

In this cumulative tale, Hattie—a big black hen—tries her best to warn her barnyard buddies that there's a fox in the bushes.

Guess What?
Illustrated by Vivienne Goodman
Harcourt Brace Jovanovich, Publisher; 1988

The personality and secret occupation of Daisy O'Grady is revealed in this unique picture book. Daisy's story is perfect for the Halloween season.

Eloise Greenfield
Famous Then—Famous Now

Eloise Greenfield remembers being famous for a whole day in fifth grade. Her teacher—despite Eloise's protests—had given her a big part in the play. But during the play, the young Eloise just couldn't get her voice to come out loud and strong. Although she delivered her lines flawlessly, not a bit of them was heard in the audience. For the rest of the day, she was famous. Everyone in the hall and on the playground knew she was the girl who couldn't speak up.

Interesting, isn't it, that time has a way of turning the tables? The girl who couldn't speak up now speaks to countless children through her poems and stories. She introduces youngsters to Black Americans including Rosa Parks, Paul Robeson, and Mary McLeod Bethune in her books. It's one of Eloise Greenfield's personal missions to make sure there is literature in which Black children can see themselves and their history. Through her characters, she models for young readers acceptable ways of dealing with conflict and solving problems. Greenfield encourages all youngsters to remember their strengths and positive qualities, even when they are faced with their own weaknesses and mistakes.

Share several of Eloise Greenfield's books with your students, and extend the experiences using the ideas in this unit.

ideas by Karen P. Shelton

She Come Bringing Me That Little Baby Girl

Illustrated by John Steptoe
Published by J. B. Lippincott Company

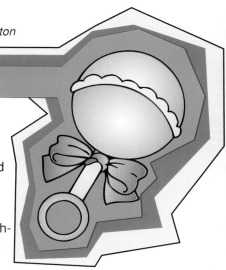

Kevin couldn't feel happy about having a baby sister. He had, after all, specifically requested a baby brother. A sister—he was sure—would never be able to play football. Read this story to your students. Then show them two gift-wrapped boxes—one pink and one blue—that are wrapped so that the lids can be removed without ripping the paper. Provide slips of paper and have students write one advantage per slip for having a baby girl in the family. Then have students repeat the process for a baby boy. Have students put their slips pertaining to baby sisters in the pink box and those pertaining to baby brothers in the blue box. Later enlist student volunteers to read aloud the slips from each box. Ask youngsters to evaluate each response to determine if it is a fact or an opinion.

Fold.

Glue.

Accordion Fold.

Our Daydreams

Daydreamers

Illustrated by Tom Feelings
Published by The Dial Press

Eloise Greenfield is a confessed daydreamer. In this poem, daydreams are given form, substance, and purpose. Discuss the author's meaning with your youngsters after reading the poem aloud to them. Ask your students to think about their daydreams. Do they "zone out," create, anticipate, plan, or ponder while they daydream? Ask each student to draw a picture of something that he daydreams about. Then have him write about the daydream and what purpose it has for him. Ask students to assist you in making a foldout booklet full of daydreams. Fold and glue a length of bulletin-board paper as shown in the illustrations. Then accordion-fold the paper. Glue the students' daydream illustrations and explanations on one or both sides of the paper. Glue a student-created cover on the front of the booklet, and glue ribbon on the back of the last page in the booklet, before folding and tying it as shown.

Grandpa's Face

Illustrated by Floyd Cooper
Published by Philomel Books

To Tamika, there's nothing quite like her grandpa's face. Its warm and loving countenance is one of the highlights of her day. Read *Grandpa's Face* to your students. Then flip back through the book, asking students to describe the grandfather's face each time it is shown. Repeat this process, having students describe Tamika's face in each illustration. Encourage each of your youngsters to contribute magazine cutouts of people's faces for a collage. Before making the collage, ask students to sort the face cutouts by expression. Which are the most pleasant? The zaniest? The saddest?

Grandmama's Joy

Illustrated by Carole Byard
Published by William Collins Publishers, Inc.

An impending move makes her grandmama very sad, even though Rhondy makes several attempts to cheer her. As children sometimes do, Rhondy helps her grandmama to remember that the most important thing is that they still have each other—even if they have a different home. After reading *Grandmama's Joy* aloud, ask your students how many of them have ever moved. Discuss the feelings of sadness that can come with a move. Then discuss some of the positive changes that can happen when people move from place to place. Have one student play the role of Grandmama while other students take turns playing the part of Rhondy. Have the Rhondy characters explain to Grandmama some of the good things about moving to a new home.

Africa Dream

Illustrated by Carole Byard
Published by The John Day Company

In this book, Eloise Greenfield takes the reader to long-ago Africa. After reading the book to your students, encourage them to find out about present-day Africa. Assist students in this endeavor by providing a mix of reference materials that can give them some appreciation of the vast diversity found on the African continent. Include materials like magazines, newspapers, travel brochures, and maps that may be cut up and used by the youngsters. Ask each student to choose a specific topic related to Africa to research. To present his report, have each student paint a large sheet of art paper to resemble African art or a textile design. When the artwork is dry, have the student fold and glue the paper to make a pocket. Have him attach a written report to the outside of the pocket and put magazine or travel-brochure pictures, newspaper clippings, or other related information inside the pocket. Staple all of the students' report pockets together beneath an appropriately decorated cover. Have each of the students in turn tell about his pocket and show what he put inside.

Nathaniel Talking

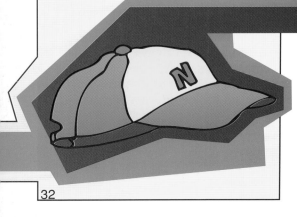

Illustrated by Jan Spivey Gilchrist
Published by Writers And Readers Publishing, Inc.

Originally Eloise Greenfield thought Nathaniel would only appear in one rap poem. But once Nathaniel came to life, he was here to stay. Share the poems in *Nathaniel Talking* with your students. Talk about the poems individually. Which ones did students like? Which ones did they not like? Ask each of your students to write a poem that has something to do with his life. Invite your young poets to share their poetry in a brief presentation. Have volunteers practice an animated rendition of "Nathaniel's Rap" to precede the original poetry readings and "Nathaniel's Rap (Reprise)" to follow the readings. When all volunteers are ready, let the rap begin!

Rave Reviews For Ruth Heller

No one makes nonfiction more appealing to children than Ruth Heller! Whether she's investigating color, parts of speech, plants, or animals, she presents the facts in a kid-pleasing style. Her secret: plenty of poetic verse, a dash of humor, and endless eye-catching illustrations. Use this collection of activities to introduce students to an amazing author and illustrator *and* an intriguing genre. No doubt both subjects will receive rave reviews from your youngsters!

ideas by Jill Hamilton, Lisa Leonardi, and Sharon Murph

◦ Meet The Author ◦

As a child Ruth Heller loved to read, draw, and color. And as an adult, she loves the same three things! Born in Canada on April 2, 1924, Heller was around the age of 11 when she moved to the United States with her family. She loved art throughout elementary, junior high, and high school; studied painting and art history in college; and returned to college to study drawing and design when her two sons were in school. Soon after, she was designing gift wrap and creating newspaper ads, posters, puzzles, and coloring books. While at an aquarium researching tropical fish for a coloring book, Heller got the idea for her first nonfiction picture book: *Chickens Aren't The Only Ones*. After several years of searching for an interested publisher, her book was published in 1981, and she's been writing and illustrating children's books ever since. To date Heller has published more than 18 nonfiction picture books—all in rhyme. Heller believes that rhyme helps children learn new facts and sophisticated vocabulary. She purposefully keeps her writing brief and plans for her illustrations to convey as much information as possible.

Heller currently resides with her husband in San Francisco. In addition to creating children's books, the author visits schools and presents at conferences for teachers and librarians. She also enjoys spending time with her family, working crossword puzzles, swimming, playing tennis, and cooking. For more information about Ruth Heller, read her autobiography *Fine Lines* (from the Meet The Author series published by Richard C. Owen Publishers, Inc.; 1996).

◦ Color ◦

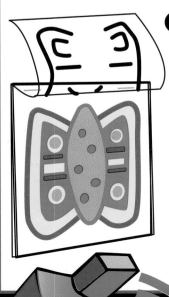

The Putnam & Grosset Group, 1995

Abracadabra! Here is just what you need to investigate the colorful pages of any book! Rhyming text, brilliant illustrations, and transparent overlays inform young readers that only four basic colors are needed to print any color in the world!

Improve your youngsters' understanding of the four-color printing process with this colorful follow-up activity. For easy management, plan to have students complete the activity at an art center under adult supervision. To begin, a student uses a yellow marker to draw and color a simple design on a five-inch square of white paper. Then he aligns a five-inch square of laminated film (or clear cellophane or acetate) atop the paper and staples the top edges. He then uses a magenta (pink or red) permanent marker to add desired color to his drawing. Next he aligns and staples a second square of laminated film atop the project and uses a cyan (blue) permanent marker to embellish his work. Finally he staples a third layer of laminated film atop his project and uses a black permanent marker to add final details. As each layer of color is added, the student witnesses additional colors being created.

This sampling of literature and the related activities explore things in nature.

Chickens Aren't The Only Ones

The Putnam & Grosset Group, 1993

Why do chickens get all the credit for laying eggs when birds, reptiles, amphibians, insects, and fish lay eggs too? Discover the size, shape, and quantity of eggs laid by several oviparous creatures in Ruth Heller's first published book.

After an oral reading of this "egg-ceptional" book, challenge students to name egg-laying animals. Divide your class into five groups and designate a recorder in each one. Give each recorder a colorful marker and a large egg cutout that you've labeled with one of the following categories: *Birds, Reptiles, Amphibians, Fish, Insects.* Then, for two or three minutes, have each group brainstorm egg-laying animals for its recorder to list on the cutout. Next have each group rotate to a different cutout along a predetermined route. Instruct each group to read the animals listed on the new cutout, then brainstorm additional names for the group's recorder to add to the list. Repeat the activity as described until every group has had the opportunity to brainstorm and list egg-laying animals for each of the five categories. Then collect the eggs and post them in a prominent classroom location. If desired post a sixth egg on which you have written the title "Mammals" and the names of the only two egg-laying mammals: "spiny anteater" and "duckbill platypus." Then, under your students' direction, attach a small egg-shaped sticker beside each correctly listed *oviparous* animal on each of the six egg cutouts.

Birds

bluebirds
owl
turkey
hen
parrot
peacock
duck
pelican
cardinal
goose
robin
blue jay

sparrow
seagull
woodpecker
eagle
penguin
toucan

Animals Born Alive And Well

The Putnam & Grosset Group, 1993

In this informative sequel to Chickens Aren't The Only Ones, *Heller fascinates her readers with a menagerie of mammals. From the largest whale to the tiniest shrew, students are introduced to more than 80 different mammals—some wild, some tame, and some prehistoric!*

Beep! Beep! Buzz! Join the electronic-pet craze with this fun follow-up activity. At the conclusion of this book, write a student-generated list of mammals on the chalkboard—at least one per student. After each child has chosen a different mammal to research, have him write his name and the name of his mammal on a white construction-paper copy of page 38. To complete the research portion of the project, the student describes his mammal's habitat and diet, and writes two or more interesting facts about the animal on the provided lines. Then he draws and colors a picture of the mammal in the box. To assemble the project, he cuts along the bold lines, folds the resulting cutout in half along the thin line, and glues the two halves together as shown. Next he hole-punches the top of the project, threads a length of yarn through the hole, and securely ties the yarn ends. A student can wear his project around his neck or tie it to his bookbag. Whichever the case, students are sure to enjoy sharing their mammal reports with their classmates. And you'll have a trendy activity that doesn't require batteries or make unwanted electronic noises!

Sam's
Mammal

zebra
(name of mammal)

LEFT   MODE   ENTER   RIGHT

Habitat
deserts and grasslands of
eastern and southern Africa

Diet
grass, bark, leaves, buds, fruits,
and roots

Interesting Facts
• No two zebras have identical
stripes
• member of the horse family
• baby zebra (foal) can stand within
an hour after birth

The Reason For A Flower

The Putnam & Grosset Group, 1992

Blossoming with information, this book examines the importance of flowers in nature. Breathtaking illustrations support an ample crop of plant-related vocabulary. This close-up look at blooms is sure to germinate plenty of interest in the plant world.

Candy from a flower? Most likely, your youngsters will be amazed by the different products that stem from flowers. Before you share this book with your students, gather classroom quantities of several products that can be traced to blooming plants, like cotton balls, popped corn, pasta pieces (uncooked), coffee beans, tea bags, rubber bands, paper scraps, twine, chocolate chips, pieces of cork, dried bread or croutons, and straw. (Each child will need six different plant products.) Then, at the conclusion of the book, have students complete the following flower-making project:

To make a flower like the one shown, a student cuts a petal shape from each of six 3" x 5" construction-paper rectangles and a leaf shape from each of two 2" x 4" construction-paper rectangles. Then he glues his six petals, a three-inch paper circle, a ten-inch paper stem, and his leaf cutouts onto a 12" x 18" sheet of construction paper to resemble a flower. When the glue has dried, he writes "Six Reasons For A Flower" in the flower's center and labels each petal with the name of a different plant product. Finally he glues a sample of each product on the corresponding petal. There's little doubt that this project will receive two thumbs-up from your youngsters—green thumbs, that is!

Once your youngsters have explored blooming plants, they'll be eager to learn about those plants that do not bloom. Ruth Heller's book, *Plants That Never Ever Bloom* (The Putnam & Grosset Group, 1984), is the perfect teaching tool!

How To Hide An Octopus And Other Sea Creatures

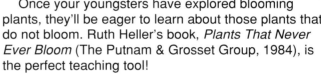

The Putnam & Grosset Group, 1992

One in a series of books about camouflage, this undersea selection features several fascinating creatures that appear to be playing hide-and-seek with readers. Delightful illustrations demonstrate how the appearances of some animals change with their surroundings, and how others rely on special patterns or colors for camouflage. It's a revealing look at the secrets of the undersea world!

For a fun follow-up to this story, have students apply their knowledge of undersea camouflage to create their own clever underwater scenes. To begin, a student draws a sea creature on colorful wallpaper or gift wrap, and cuts it out. Then she glues this cutout to a sheet of light blue construction paper and uses crayons or markers to create a background scene that camouflages the creature. Mount the students' undersea scenes on a bulletin board titled "Hide-And-Seek Beneath The Sea." Students will have a grand time trying to find their classmates' camouflaged creatures.

If your students enjoyed this book, they're sure to enjoy other books in Ruth Heller's How To Hide series:
- *How To Hide A Polar Bear And Other Mammals*
  The Putnam & Grosset Group, 1994

- *How To Hide A Butterfly And Other Insects*
  The Putnam & Grosset Group, 1992

- *How To Hide A Meadow Frog And Other Amphibians*
  The Putnam & Grosset Group, 1995

- *How To Hide A Parakeet And Other Birds*
  The Putnam & Grosset Group, 1995

- *How To Hide A Crocodile And Other Reptiles*
  The Putnam & Grosset Group, 1994

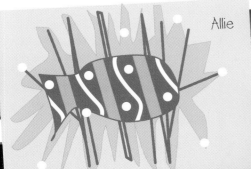

Studying The Parts Of Speech

When Ruth Heller made a promise to write a book about each part of speech, she became a teacher's best friend! The following books—each accompanied by a classroom-tested idea—are from the author's Parts-Of-Speech series.

A Cache Of Jewels And Other Collective Nouns

The Putnam & Grosset Group, 1998

In this informative book, Ruth Heller uses a bevy *of beautiful illustrations to portray a* clutch *of collective nouns!*

Delight your brood with this gem of an activity. After an oral reading of the book, write a phrase on the chalkboard that includes a collective noun. Then invite students to provide additional phrases that feature collective nouns, and list their ideas. Next give each child a white construction-paper copy of the treasure-chest pattern on page 39. To complete the project, a student writes and illustrates a different collective-noun phrase in each numbered section of the pattern. Then he cuts on the bold outer lines, carefully cuts along the short dotted line, and glues the two resulting cutouts together where indicated. While the glue is drying, he folds forward the top and bottom sections of his project along the thin lines and uses crayons or markers to decorate the blank surfaces to resemble a treasure chest. Then the student accordion-folds the project along the remaining thin lines and inserts the tab into the slit as shown on the "Finished Project." Be sure to set aside time for youngsters to share their completed projects with their classmates.

1. army of ants
2. fleet of ships
3. string of pearls
4. school of fish

Many Luscious Lollipops: A Book About Adjectives

The Putnam & Grosset Group, 1992

"An ADJECTIVE's terrific when you want to be specific." Through imaginative text and lively illustrations, Ruth Heller presents an array of adjectives that are sure to delight your young audience and educate them too!

Adjectives can describe any number of nouns or pronouns; but for this kid-pleasing follow-up activity, each student must describe a very special noun: herself! To begin have each student trace both of her hands on a sheet of skin-toned paper, then cut out the shapes. Next instruct each youngster to write a different, self-describing adjective on each finger and thumb of her cutouts. To complete the project, she uses desired arts-and-crafts supplies—like fabric scraps, construction paper, yarn, markers, crayons, and glue—to create a likeness of herself on a 12" x 18" sheet of construction paper. Then she glues her hand cutouts to the project as shown.

To extend the activity, collect the completed projects, read aloud the adjectives each student wrote, and challenge the class to identify this classmate. Then showcase the projects in the school hallway where others can see your *super, wonderful,* and *talented* students!

Kites Sail High: A Book About Verbs

The Putnam & Grosset Group, 1988

Open the cover of this book, and you find a wonderful world of verbs just waiting to be discovered! From action to linking to tenses to moods, an array of verbs and verb types are highlighted. By the conclusion of this book, your youngsters are sure to agree that verbs are most superb!

Your students' knowledge of verbs is sure to soar with this action-verb activity. At the conclusion of the book, have each student make a list of ten or more actions that he does during a normal day, like *eat, talk, sit,* and *laugh.* (Accept all verb tenses.) Then have each student draw a tic-tac-toe grid on a nine-inch square of white paper. Have each child use a crayon or marker to write his name in the center square. Then, in each of the remaining squares, instruct each student to write a different action verb from his list and create a corresponding illustration. Have each child mount his completed project on a colorful ten-inch square of construction paper; then display the projects on a bulletin board labeled "We're Ready For Action!"

Behind The Mask: A Book About Prepositions

The Putnam & Grosset Group, 1995

So just exactly what is the purpose of a preposition? This playful and eye-pleasing exploration reveals that this part of speech tells us the when, where, and how of things!

What would the English language be like without prepositions? To help youngsters understand the importance of this part of speech in their daily conversations, challenge the class to a game of No Prepositions, Please. Select one student volunteer to begin the first round of play, and whisper the name of a classroom item in this student's ear. The object of the game is for this student to give his classmates clues about the location of the mystery item without naming the item or using any prepositions. If a classmate identifies the mystery item and its location, the class earns a point. If the player names the item or uses a preposition, the teacher scores a point, and the round of play is over. Play the game until the message is clear: prepositions are a very important part of speech!

More Parts-Of-Speech Books

If your students enjoy the books on pages 36 and 37, they're sure to enjoy the other books in this series:

*   *Merry-Go-Round: A Book About Nouns*
    The Putnam & Grosset Group, 1992

*   *Up, Up, And Away: A Book About Adverbs*
    The Putnam & Grosset Group, 1993

*   *Mine, All Mine!: A Book About Pronouns*
    The Putnam & Grosset Group, 1997

*   *Fantastic And Wow!: A Book About Interjections And Conjunctions*
    The Putnam & Grosset Group, 1998

Pattern

Use with *Animals Born Alive And Well* on page 34.

's

Mammal

RIGHT

ENTER

MODE

LEFT

(name of mammal)

Habitat

Diet

Interesting Facts

Use with *A Cache Of Jewels...* on page 36.

Strip A

tab

Collective Nouns

by _____

1.

2.

Finished Project

Strip B

Glue to Strip A.

3.

4.

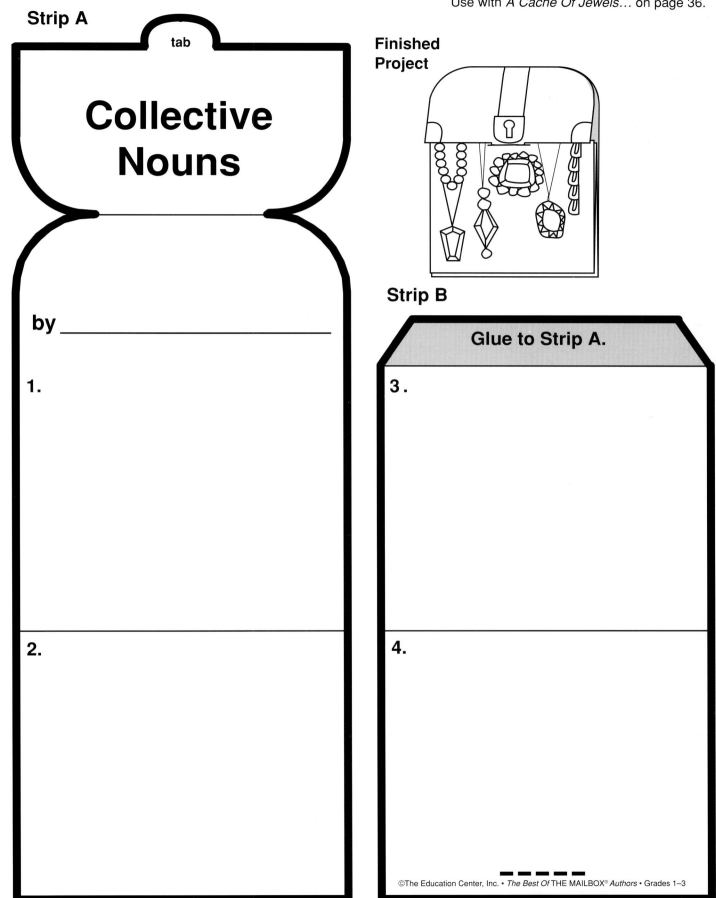

©The Education Center, Inc. • *The Best Of* THE MAILBOX® *Authors* • Grades 1–3

Back To School With Kevin Henkes

Kevin Henkes took a brave step at a young age. Carrying three portfolios filled with artwork and a children's book that he'd written and illustrated, the college freshman flew to New York City in search of a publisher. His search was short and sweet—his

first official appointment landed him a book contract. Not bad for a 19-year-old kid from Wisconsin!

Kevin, the second-youngest in a family of four children, showed an interest in art at an early age. Drawing on anything from tiny scraps of paper to the backs of discarded envelopes, Kevin enjoyed creating pictures, and others enjoyed his creations. He also loved to read and looked forward to the regular trips he made with his family to the local library. His love for children's books resurfaced during high school when he became interested in writing. As soon as he realized that children's books were a combination of the two things that he most enjoyed—illustration and writing—he knew without a doubt what his career goal would be.

Henkes modestly attributes a large amount of his success to the support he continues to receive from his family and friends, and to the guidance he receives from a top-notch editor who asks all the right questions. This is from a man who seeks perfection and pushes himself to attain it, an author and illustrator who captures with his words and pictures the hurdles and triumphs of childhood, and a kid-at-heart who has a delightful sense of irrepressible humor.

Henkes's advice to aspiring writers is: "Everyone has stories to tell. If you want to write, look at your own experiences. Don't worry about creating masterpieces. Don't worry if your work is not perfect. Rewrite and keep working. Just because someone is published does not mean it comes easily. Enjoy what you are doing. Have fun!"

And having fun is exactly what's in store for you and your youngsters! Use the ideas on the next five pages to follow up several of Kevin Henkes's stories. We feel certain a good time will be had by all.

ideas contributed by Theresa Ives Audet

Bailey Goes Camping

Greenwillow Books, 1985

What does a little bunny named Bailey do when his older brother and sister go on a Bunny Scout camping trip and leave him behind? After a bit of bunny pouting and some encouragement from his folks, he has a terrific time eating hot dogs, fishing in the bathtub, and roasting marshmallows!

If this story were to continue, Bailey would eventually write and illustrate a delightful children's book about his camping adventures as a youngster. That's what author Kevin Henkes did! You see, the story *Bailey Goes Camping* is based on a childhood memory of being left behind while two older brothers went camping. Many of your students with older siblings will empathize with Bailey. Even students without older siblings have probably fallen victim to the "you're just too young," and "When you get a little older…," explanations that adults often offer as to why certain requests cannot be honored. For a fun follow-up to this story, enlist your students in mixing up a batch of trail mix (any combination of raisins, peanuts, cereal, dried fruit, and candy pieces). As students munch on servings of this tasty camping snack, invite them to talk about things they have asked to do, that their parents wouldn't be talked into. Have the students evaluate why they felt their requests should have been granted. Also ask students to recall the antics that they used to try to convince their parents to agree to their requests. Have students brainstorm how they might make the best of these disappointing situations in the future—now that they've heard Bailey's story.

Grandpa & Bo

Greenwillow Books, 1986

This heartwarming story is a gentle reminder of the important role grandparents play in children's lives. While Bo spends the summer with his grandpa, the twosome do many things together. They fish, take long walks, and even celebrate Christmas! And when at last the youngster and his grandpa spy a shooting star, it seems perfectly natural that their wishes would be exactly the same.

Close by or faraway, grandparents love without restrictions and with endless patience. Their experiences and wisdom open the past to the eager ears and open hearts of a younger generation. Invite students to talk about special times that they have spent with their grandparents or other older adults. Follow up the discussion by having each student design a brag book about a favorite older person. To do this, give each child a construction-paper mini-booklet containing four to six blank pages. The student decorates and personalizes the front cover of his brag booklet. On the first booklet page, he writes a dedication to the person to whom he plans on giving the completed mini-booklet. On each of the following pages, he describes a special trait of the older adult or he writes about a special memory that the twosome have shared. The recipients of these projects will thank their lucky stars to have such thoughtful young admirers.

The topic of shooting stars—those streaks of light that have long fascinated sky watchers—is sure to evoke an enthusiastic response from your youngsters. Ask students to share their knowledge and questions about shooting stars. Then inform students that some people believe that a wish made upon a shooting star is a wish that will come true. For a fun writing activity, have each youngster design a page for a class booklet of shooting-star wishes. To make a booklet page, fold a sheet of 9" x 12" construction paper in half and glue the outer edges to form a pocket. Draw and color a night sky scene on the front of the pocket, and personalize the back of the pocket. Then, on a slip of paper, have each student write and personalize his wish for a shooting star and tuck it inside the pocket. Bind the pockets between a construction-paper cover labeled "Shooting-Star Wishes." Place the completed project in your classroom library for all to enjoy.

A Weekend With Wendell

Greenwillow Books, 1986

Things run amok when Wendell, a mischievous mouse, spends the weekend at Sophie's house. From making all the rules (none of which are fair) to giving Sophie a new shaving-cream hairdo, Wendell is up to no good. Even Sophie's parents are dismayed at the rebellious rodent. But in the end, Sophie surprises Wendell with a trick of her own, and a new friendship unfolds.

After reading this story aloud, poll your class to find out which students have been on sleepovers. Invite students to talk about their sleepover experiences. What do they think are the most fun parts of a sleepover? The scariest parts? Then have each student pack a bag for an imaginary sleepover. To do this, have each child fold and cut a 9" x 12" sheet of construction paper as shown to create a suitcase cutout. Staple four sheets of writing paper inside the suitcase. Have the students label their sheets with the following headings: "Things I Must Pack," "A Scary Story I'll Tell," "Three Things I Must Remember To Do," and "Three Things I Must Remember Not To Do." Allow plenty of time for students to complete their pages and decorate the outsides of their suitcases. Then have each youngster label a piece of 2" x 3" construction paper with his name and address and attach the tag to his suitcase handle using a hole puncher and a length of ribbon. Students will enjoy sharing these projects with their classmates and their families.

Once Around The Block

illustrated by Victoria Chess
Greenwillow Books, 1987
(This book is out of print. Check with your library.)
Annie is bored, so her mother tells her to take a walk around the block. This wise advice starts Annie on a journey that fills her afternoon with fun and excitement.

Most youngsters can easily recall times when they have felt bored and could think of nothing to do. This easy-to-make project puts a stop to boredom! To begin, divide students into small groups. Ask each group to brainstorm a list of things that children their ages can do by themselves. When the allotted time is over, have each group share its ideas. Compile the ideas on the chalkboard and entitle the resulting list "Boredom Busters." Next give each child five to ten large index cards. Ask each student to choose his favorite Boredom Busters from the list and write each one on a different index card. To record additional Boredom Busters, suggest that students use the backs of their cards. Finally give each child two large index cards to personalize and decorate for front and back covers. To complete the project, have each student hole-punch the upper left-hand corner of each of his cards and thread a metal ring or something similar through the holes. Encourage students to take their projects home and store them for safekeeping. When boredom strikes, who are they going to call? The Boredom Busters!

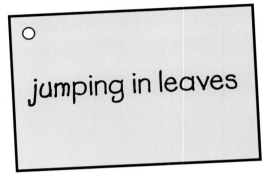

Sheila Rae, The Brave

Greenwillow Books, 1987

Sheila Rae is brave. She is fearless. But when she tries to walk home from school a different way than usual—she is lost! The unexpected heroine in this tale of two mice is none other than Sheila Rae's scaredy-cat little sister. In this adorable story, two mouse sisters learn about bravery, each other, and themselves.

Once students have heard Sheila Rae and Louise's story, they'll most likely be eager to talk about times when they have felt afraid. Encourage students to share their experiences and explain how they dealt with their fears. Then, using a comic-strip format, have each student create a personalized story about bravery. To make a comic strip, fold a 12" x 18" sheet of construction paper in half and crease it. Repeat this two more times; then unfold the paper to reveal eight rectangles. To complete his comic strip, a student illustrates a sequence of events that tells a story in which he faces—and then overcomes—a fearful situation. Once students have shared their completed projects with their classmates, collect the comic strips and publish them in a newspaper format. To do this, cut and fold several lengths of bulletin-board paper to resemble blank newspaper pages. Decorate the front page to show the title "Special Edition: Overcoming Fears," the date, and a class byline. Mount your students' completed projects, two per page, on the folded paper. Laminate the pages for durability; then place the resulting newspaper in your class library for all to read. Extra! Extra! Read all about it!

Chester's Way

Greenwillow Books, 1988

Chester has a certain way of doing things. His friend Wilson does things just like he does, and that makes Chester happy. Then Lilly, a one-of-a-kind mouse, moves into their neighborhood. She doesn't do anything like anyone else, and that makes Chester very uncomfortable. Eventually Chester learns to embrace Lilly's uniqueness and actually finds himself changing under her zany influence. It isn't hard to understand how Lilly has become one of Kevin Henkes's favorite characters. Her self-assuredness and eccentricity are endearing. Henkes breaks stereotypes by giving the female character the derring-do and unabashed courage to break conventions.

After reading aloud *Chester's Way,* ask students to recall the things that Lilly and Chester taught one another. Also ask students to think of things they've learned from friends who have enriched their lives. Help students understand that people (and mice!) learn from each other. Then plan a day on which each student demonstrates for her classmates a special skill, talent, or interest that she has. For example a child might demonstrate how to tie a double knot in a shoestring, braid hair, fold paper to make shapes, or do the splits. For a surprise treat at the conclusion of the demonstrations, provide the supplies needed to make peanut butter-and-jelly sandwiches. And don't forget to bring some cookie cutters! Your youngsters can cut shapes from their sandwiches with the cookie cutters, just as Lilly would do. Your children will see that they too can learn from the irrepressible Lilly.

Chester learns that he should not judge others just because they do things differently than he does. In fact, he discovers that making friends and learning new things are loads of fun. With this in mind, find out how your students think Chester and his pals will embrace Victor, the newest member of their neighborhood. For writing motivation, show students the final illustration in the book; then have each child write a sequel to *Chester's Way* that stars Victor as the new kid on the block. Suggest that students describe Victor's unique traits and talents; explain how Chester, Wilson, and Lilly meet Victor; and tell about an adventure the foursome share.

Julius, The Baby Of The World

Greenwillow Books, 1990

The irrepressible Lilly is back and this time she's kicking up her red boots over the latest addition to her family—her brother Julius. Before the baby arrives, Lilly is the best big sister in the world. But after Julius—the baby of the world—is born, Lilly decides her new brother is indeed the biggest pain in the world. This hilarious story of intense sibling rivalry was actually inspired by Henkes's real-life nieces. Imagine that!

At the conclusion of the story, ask students how they feel about Lilly's experience. Did they learn anything from Lilly? Have they ever felt similar feelings? If so, how did they cope with their feelings of jealousy? When the students have finished sharing their ideas, they'll be ready to complete this "Best In The World" project. Draw a globe pattern similar to the one shown below; then duplicate a class supply on white construction paper. On the chalkboard write "[student's name], The _____ Of The World." Ask each child to decide how to complete the title. For example, a child might choose to be the sister, brother, student, helper, or athlete of the world. Then distribute the globe patterns, and ask each student to copy and complete the title and illustrate himself in the role he chose (see the illustration). After adding any other desired decorations, have students cut out and mount their projects onto black construction paper. Display the completed projects on a bulletin board entitled "The Best In The World!"

Joey Smith
The Basketball Player
Of The World

Chrysanthemum
Greenwillow Books, 1991

Chrysanthemum absolutely loves her name—until her first day of school! As soon as Chrysanthemum's classmates hear her name, the teasing begins. Though her parents assure their daughter that her name is as perfect as she is, the teasing continues and the young mouse is mortified. When it seems as if there's no hope for a mouse with a flower name, Mrs. Delphinium Twinkle enters the picture.

An afternoon jog provided Henkes with the inspiration for Chrysanthemum's story. It was near the end of his run that the author observed a young girl being teased by her peers. The forlorn look on the young girl's face reminded Henkes of a kindergarten memory of his own. These experiences materialized into the young mouse's story.

After reading the story aloud, ask your students to share what they know about their names. Do they know who named them or whom they were named after? For a fun, family-centered homework activity, ask students to interview their parents to find out more about their names. If desired, give each child a copy of the interview questions on page 45. When the sheets have been returned, invite each student to share two or three facts that he learned about his "absolutely perfect" name!

Even children who love their names may wonder what it would be like to have a different name. Why not let them find out for themselves? Tell students that for one day they may change their names. Encourage students to choose names that they feel match their personalities and interests. Then, on a strip of construction paper, have each student design a nametag that reflects his new name. For added fun, collect the nametags and display them one at a time, challenging the students to guess whom each new name belongs to. Then have the students attach their nametags to their desks for the day. For a fun graphing activity, create a class graph that shows how many students chose to name themselves for famous people, relatives, colors, flowers, or friends. What's in a name? Plenty of opportunities for learning!

Owen
Greenwillow Books, 1993

Owen has a favorite blanket. He has loved it, stained it, and worn it threadbare. And he refuses—much to his parents' disdain—to discard it. Finally, Owen's mom finds a comforting way to solve the blanket dilemma. Owen's story will be reassuring to those youngsters who find it difficult to give up favorite items.

After reading the story to your class, tell students about a favorite blanket, stuffed toy, or other object that you had as a child. Describe the item and explain to students why it was important to you. Then invite students to talk about their most-loved items. Follow up the discussion with a quilt-making activity that would make Owen proud! On a nine-inch square of drawing paper, have each student illustrate a much-loved item that he hopes to have forever. Collect the squares and mount them on a bulletin board covered in yellow paper, leaving approximately two inches between the illustrations. Then use a marker to draw "stitches" around the projects. If desired, attach gathered crepe paper to the outer edges of the display for a quilt border, and add the title "Our Favorite Things."

Put your students' creative-thinking skills to the test with this small-group activity. Read *Owen* to your class a second time, stopping just after Owen's mother has "an absolutely wonderful, positively perfect, especially terrific idea." Challenge each group of students to brainstorm ideas for redesigning the blanket into a more acceptable form. Then have each group choose its favorite idea and present it to the class. If desired, take a class vote to find out the favorite blanket-transforming idea. Who knows? You may find that your youngsters' ideas are just as handy as the handkerchiefs!

Investigating My Name

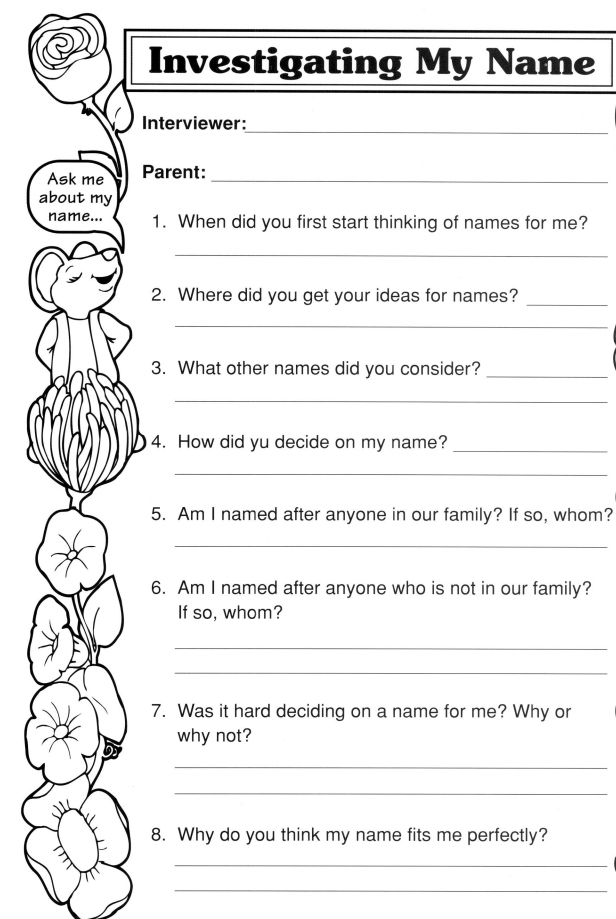

Interviewer: _____

Parent: _____

1. When did you first start thinking of names for me?
   _____

2. Where did you get your ideas for names? _____
   _____

3. What other names did you consider? _____
   _____

4. How did yu decide on my name? _____
   _____

5. Am I named after anyone in our family? If so, whom?
   _____

6. Am I named after anyone who is not in our family? If so, whom?
   _____
   _____

7. Was it hard deciding on a name for me? Why or why not?
   _____
   _____

8. Why do you think my name fits me perfectly?
   _____
   _____

Note To Teacher: Use with "Chrysanthemum" on page 44.

Tony Johnston

Teacher Turned Author

Pick and choose from this sampling of Tony Johnston's work and the related classroom activities.

About The Author

As a youngster, Tony collected everything that crawled or flew. She even raised Monarch butterflies! But her childhood dream of becoming a veterinarian or a "bugologist" was replaced by other interests. Soon after graduating from Stanford University, Tony Johnston began teaching elementary school. Her love of writing was apparent in the stories that she wrote for her students. At the urging of a fellow teacher, Johnston investigated getting her stories published. It was an investigation that took time and energy, but one that young readers today are thankful for. To date, Johnston has published nearly 75 books and has plenty more on tap. She currently resides in California.

The Quilt Story
Illustrated by Tomie dePaola
G. P. Putnam's Sons, 1985
Follow a well-loved quilt through the years and across the miles as it provides warmth and comfort to those who love it.

After reading this book aloud, discuss how the quilt helped both of the girls in the story. Share with students an example of something that brought you warmth and comfort as a child, such as a favorite quilt, blanket, stuffed toy, or special place. To make a class quilt that is overflowing with warm feelings, ask each child to illustrate his special item or favorite place on a nine-inch square of white construction paper. Mount the illustrations on a bulletin board covered with brightly colored paper, leaving about two inches between the illustrations. Then use a marker to draw stitches around the project. If desired, attach gathered crepe paper to the outer edges of the display for a quilt border.

Whale Song
Illustrated by Ed Young
G. P. Putnam's Sons, 1987
A procession of impressive whales sing their way through ocean waters, passing on to one another the numbers from one to ten.

Could these gentle giants gliding through the world's oceans really be counting to one another? This poetic tale is sure to please your youngsters and invoke some creative thoughts as well. At the conclusion of the story, ask your youngsters to share what they know about whales and what they'd like to find out. Then make plans to study these one-of-a-kind mammals. For a fun writing activity, have each child write and illustrate a make-believe story about what else whales might be conversing about underwater. Compile the stories into a whale-shaped booklet like the one shown.

Grandpa's Song

Illustrated by Brad Sneed
Dial Books For Young Readers, 1991

Grandpa—a big, round man with a bellowing voice—is shaken when he forgets the words to his favorite song. But his grandchildren are there to carry the tune in a joyous expression of love that's as big and strong as Grandpa's voice.

Like the hero of this story, Tony Johnston's grandfather once composed a song that everyone in the family had to learn! Discuss Grandpa and what a character he is. Ask students if they know of anyone who reminds them of Grandpa in one way or another. Also talk about why Grandpa has trouble remembering things; then ask students to suggest ways they can help older people who have similar problems. For a fun finale, have your students follow your lead as you assume Grandpa's singing stance. Then, as a class, belt out a few favorite tunes!

The Cowboy And The Black-Eyed Pea

Illustrated by Warren Ludwig
G. P. Putnam's Sons, 1992

In this clever parody of The Princess And The Pea, *the wealthy daughter of a Texas rancher devises a plan to find a real cowboy among her many suitors.*

Follow up an oral reading of this story by reading aloud your favorite version of *The Princess And The Pea*. Divide students into small groups and ask each group to compare the two stories, then create a list of similarities and a list of differences. Compile the group lists into a class list. To conclude the activity, have students vote for the tale that they like the best.

Karen Cast—Gr. 2, Ben Milam Elementary, Cameron, TX

Saddle up for some superb storytelling with this creative-writing activity. First discuss the many qualities that a cowboy must have, like being strong, hardworking, and brave—as well as being sensitive to environmental concerns, and the needs of people and animals. Then have each student describe and illustrate her ideas for the most comfortable saddle in the world. Be sure to set aside time for students to share their inventions with their classmates.

Carole Curcio—Gr. 1, Hampton School, Hampton, NJ

Slither McCreep
And His Brother, Joe

Illustrated by Victoria Chess
Harcourt Brace Jovanovich, Publishers; 1992

Slither, a young snake, is furious that his brother, Joe, won't share his toys. Determined to get even, Slither sneaks into Joe's room and squeezes Joe's toys until they break. However, instead of satisfaction, Slither feels remorseful about his squeezing rampage.

When this project is complete, your youngsters can have a hissy-fit of giggles too! To make a Slither McCreep look-alike, each student draws a large snake shape on a sheet of 12" x 18" drawing paper. Then, following your oral directions, the student draws and colors a series of geometric shapes inside his snake outline. When the projects are complete, ask students to recall how Slither felt after his squeezing frenzy and how the two brothers came to terms with what had happened. Encourage students to talk about times they have done things that they later wished they hadn't.

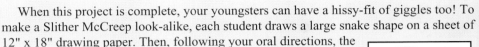

Carrie Rensberger, Angleton, TX

Lorenzo, The Naughty Parrot

Illustrated by Leo Politi
Harcourt Brace Jovanovich, Publishers; 1992

Wherever the action is—or wherever the cookies are—that's where you'll find Lorenzo. He's a watchdog pet parrot who gets into lots of trouble trying to protect his human family.

Lorenzo is a busy parrot! With the help of your students, recap the events of each of Lorenzo's four adventures. Have students identify how Lorenzo finds trouble each time. Is it his curiosity that lands him in trouble? His tendency to be overprotective? Or both? Invite students to share pet-related stories that have landed other pets in trouble. Then have each child write and illustrate another adventure for Lorenzo. When the projects are complete, bind them into a classroom book titled "Lorenzo's Latest Adventures." A few days later, gather your youngsters around you and read the stories aloud while your youngsters munch on Lorenzo's favorite snack—cookies!

The Tale Of Rabbit And Coyote

Illustrated by Tomie dePaola
G. P. Putnam's Sons, 1994

If you think a man resides in the moon, look again! In this Zapotec retelling, Rabbit coaxes Coyote into a series of disasters—then scampers to the moon where he is safely out of reach.

Poor Coyote! He's such a gullible pup that Rabbit outwits him time and time again. Read the story aloud a second time, stopping after each incident. Ask students what Coyote could have done to thwart each of Rabbit's clever plans. Next ask students how they think Coyote might be able to get Rabbit back from the moon. Brainstorm ideas as a class; then use the ideas to compose a class story. To make a big book titled "Clever Coyote," copy the resulting story text onto a series of large story pages. As a class, determine a color scheme for the book; then have students work together to illustrate the story pages before compiling them into a big book.

Amber On The Mountain

Illustrated by Robert Duncan
Dial Books For Young Readers, 1994

Amber's mountain is a beautiful yet lonely place until she meets Anna—a girl from the city. As a wonderful friendship unfolds between the two girls, Anna helps Amber realize that anything is possible "if you fix your mind on it"—and that includes learning to read and write.

At the conclusion of this heartwarming story, discuss Amber's determination. Invite students to talk about times that they have set goals, and then—when the going got rough—gave up on their goals and themselves. Also discuss the challenges that Amber faced and the support she received from Anna. Then, on a strip of white construction paper, have each student write a goal that she is ready to fix her mind on. The goals may be personalized or anonymous. Mount the programmed strips on a bulletin board that students have decorated to resemble Amber's mountain paradise. Title the display "Our Minds Are Fixed!"

Barbara Denlinger—Grs. K–2 Reading Teacher, Bergstrasse Elementary School, Ephrata, PA

The Old Lady And The Birds

Illustrated by Stephanie Garcia
Harcourt Brace And Company, 1994

In her garden in Mexico, a weathered Mexican woman passes the hours in harmony with her garden. She is alone—but never forlorn—in this touching story of kindness.

Tony Johnston lived in Mexico for 15 years. She spent many hours in beautiful enclosed gardens, watching birds and listening to fountains. No doubt these experiences influenced her as she wrote this touching tale. Have students recall the ways in which the old lady watches out and cares for the birds. Discuss the joy that she experiences from spending time in her garden and ask students if they think the woman feels alone there. Then have each child write a letter to the old lady in which he describes a beautiful, bird-filled garden that he would like for her to visit. In his letter the student can explain the kinds of things that the lady could see and do in the special garden. Students who finish early can illustrate the garden paradises that they've described!

The Iguana Brothers

Illustrated by Mark Teague
The Blue Sky Press, 1995

Dom and Tom, two iguana brothers living in Mexico, crawl through three laid-back adventures. After several bouts of thinking—followed by long hours of lazing in the sun—the duo discover that brothers make terrific best friends.

What is a best friend? List your students' ideas on the chalkboard. Be sure that the student-generated list reflects friendship tips from the iguana brothers. For a fun follow-up activity, have each student design an eye-catching poster that includes three or more pointers for being a good friend. Display the friendship posters throughout your school. Wouldn't Dom and Tom be impressed?

Steven Kellogg

Born With A Picture In His Head And A Crayon In His Hand

by Karen P. Shelton

*S*teven Kellogg once told an audience that he was born with a picture in his head and a crayon in his hand. Before he was old enough to go to school, Kellogg had made up his mind to make his artwork the focus of his career. Once you glance inside one of his picture books, it's easy to believe that he's a person who has nurtured his artistic talent most of his life. It's also easy to believe that he started concocting and illustrating stories in his childhood. With a stack of paper in his lap and a pencil in his hand, the young Kellogg sat between his younger sisters, drawing as he talked his way through one story episode after another. Each time a page was fully illustrated, he'd pass the page to one of the girls. According to Kellogg's accounts, each storytelling session continued until his sisters became restless, or until they were buried beneath the sheets of paper.

Today, if you sit in on one of Steven Kellogg's school presentations, you'll find that he rattles off a tale in much the same manner as he did in his childhood. But, instead of having a sister on his left and another on his right, there are apt to be a few dozen children on his left and a few dozen more on his right. His pads of plain white paper are colossal. But as he rapidly wields a marker across the pages, the sheets come alive with detail after glorious detail. In much the same way that the pages come alive with the touch of his marker, the air becomes alive with the dialogue of his characters—the tones of which can range from a high-pitched diminutive mouse squeak to the deep, booming bellow of a braggart. He brings to his stories the kind of theatrical zeal that makes one wonder if—at a flourish of his hand—he couldn't command the ocean waves from his illustrations to crash down on his audience. When the story is done, masterpieces lie on the floor around him, echoes of his voice fade away, and the audience will never again be able to recall that story without a feeling of awe.

Bring the imaginative world of Steven Kellogg's books to your youngsters using the following suggestions for books that he both wrote and illustrated.

From **PREHISTORIC PINKERTON** by **Steven Kellogg.** Copyright ©1987 by Steven Kellogg. Used by permission of Dial Books For Young Readers, a division of Penguin Putnam Inc.

Can I Keep Him?

Published by The Dial Press

Can I Keep Him?, one of Steven Kellogg's first books, is a bit autobiographical. As a child Kellogg was always bringing home some sort of creature in an effort to persuade his unrelenting parents to let him keep it. In desperation, he even tried to adopt the pets of his neighbors that already had perfectly good homes. Perhaps this is a dilemma some of your youngsters will be able to relate to.

After reading aloud *Can I Keep Him?*, give each child a sheet of paper printed front and back as shown. Ask each youngster to choose a different animal for his subject. (Or have each student pull a labeled strip from a cleaned pet-food can to determine his subject.) Have each child complete the sentence and draw an illustration of the creature on the front of his sheet. Then have him complete the sentence on the back of the page and draw a picture of the creature in the process of committing the predicted offense(s). Create one page that says, "I found these friends at school. Can I keep them?" Attach a class photo to the bottom of the page, and write the word "yes" on the back of the page. Stack the class photo page beneath the students' pages and staple them between student-decorated covers bearing the title "Can We Keep Them?"

I found a
walrus
Can I keep him?

No, you can't keep him because his tusks would tear the carpet.

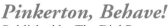

Pinkerton, Behave!

Published by The Dial Press

Here's another of Kellogg's books with the roots of the story deeply embedded in some of his real-life experiences. Kellogg, who got the *real* Pinkerton as a puppy, described the Great Dane as wonderful, stubborn, perverse, crazy, and impossible to train—but also as innocent, totally lovable, and irresistible! Your youngsters will agree that Pinkerton is irresistible after you read aloud *Pinkerton, Behave!* After such a lead-in, your youngsters will be eager to tell stories about the misbehaviors of their pets.

Enlist the help of your students in making this talking bulletin-board display and in filling it with real and/or make-believe stories about their stubborn, perverse, and impossible pets. Have students tear large areas from folded sheets of newspaper and staple both the unfolded sheets and the torn bits to a bulletin board covered in black paper. Position a large photo or drawing of a Great Dane's head so that it appears to be peeking from one of the holes. Use two sizes of potato halves to stamp giant black pawprints randomly on the board. Title the board "BEHAVE!" Ask each child to attach to the board a picture or drawing of the pet whose misbehavior he will tell about. Number the drawings. Then record each student's voice as he tells the number of his pet and recounts its misadventures. Place the tape, tape recorder, and headphones on a table beneath the board, and encourage students to listen in their spare time.

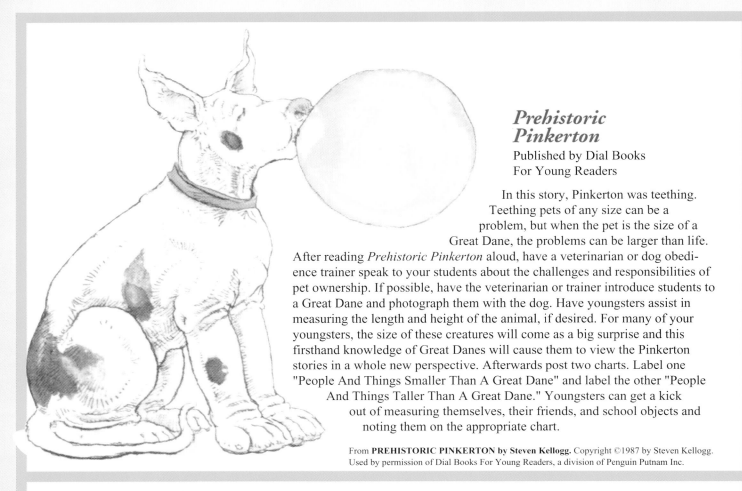

Prehistoric Pinkerton

Published by Dial Books
For Young Readers

In this story, Pinkerton was teething. Teething pets of any size can be a problem, but when the pet is the size of a Great Dane, the problems can be larger than life. After reading *Prehistoric Pinkerton* aloud, have a veterinarian or dog obedience trainer speak to your students about the challenges and responsibilities of pet ownership. If possible, have the veterinarian or trainer introduce students to a Great Dane and photograph them with the dog. Have youngsters assist in measuring the length and height of the animal, if desired. For many of your youngsters, the size of these creatures will come as a big surprise and this firsthand knowledge of Great Danes will cause them to view the Pinkerton stories in a whole new perspective. Afterwards post two charts. Label one "People And Things Smaller Than A Great Dane" and label the other "People And Things Taller Than A Great Dane." Youngsters can get a kick out of measuring themselves, their friends, and school objects and noting them on the appropriate chart.

A Rose For Pinkerton

Published by The Dial Press

The Kellogg household is a sanctuary for numerous dogs and cats. The senior cat in the family, Secondhand Rose, provided the inspiration for *A Rose For Pinkerton* by harassing everyone in the world, including Pinkerton. After reading aloud *A Rose For Pinkerton,* ask each student to contribute to a collection of magazine pictures and drawings of cats for a classroom Castle of the Cats. Encourage them to include cartoon cats as well as realistic ones. While you're waiting for your cat picture collection to grow, construct a tabletop castle from eight empty oatmeal containers and a box—but don't yet connect the pieces. Have students work cooperatively to create a collage of cats on each of the castle construction pieces. When the collages are complete and dry, use clear packing tape to hold the pieces in place. To the upper edges of the turrets and the castle walls, attach strips of paper that have been trimmed into tongue-and-groove shapes.

Once the castle is complete, have each student select a cat pictured on the castle. Then, on a sheet of paper trimmed to resemble a banner, have him write about the attitude of the cat and what kinds of things he's likely to get into as a result of his attitude. Mount the completed projects on construction paper; then trim this paper to create an eye-catching border. Attach students' papers to the edges of the table. Have students read the banners and try to determine which cat of the castle each writer described.

Much Bigger Than Martin
Published by The Dial Press

   Kellogg knows from firsthand experience the disappointments of living in a world filled with Martins. *Much Bigger Than Martin* is his way of passing the word that a person is only as insignificant as he feels.

   Read aloud *Much Bigger Than Martin* and find out what personal experiences your students have had that make them feel like Henry did. Then display the back of the book and discuss with your youngsters the picture of the cat and his image of himself. Have each student find or draw a picture of someone or something wimpy, ordinary, or seemingly insignificant. Then have him draw an illustration of what that person's or thing's imagined self-image is. If desired, have students write about these grandiose images, and bind the pictures and writings into a book titled "Not Much Bigger Than Me."

The Island Of The Skog
Published by Dial Books For Young Readers

   When you read *The Island Of The Skog* to your students, be sure to use low, booming, abrasive voices for Bouncer and the Rowdies and higher, gentler ones for Jenny, Louise, and Hannah. Steven Kellogg does. So be dramatic! And if a colleague catches you in midact, just say that's the way the author does it.

   On the day you plan to read this story, draw a banner bearing the words "National Rodent Day" on the chalkboard. Before your story time, write the word *Skog* on the board, and ask each youngster to draw what a Skog looks like. Just prior to reading the story, serve each youngster a wedge of cheese on which to nibble. Once the story has been read, ask youngsters to recall why the mice left their home. Then ask why the Skog was afraid of the mice and why the mice had terrorized the Skog. Point out that most conflicts can be handled when the two parties get together and try to reach a compromise. Show students some newspaper articles about local, state, national, and international conflicts, and explain the gists of the conflicts. Have students role-play ways to resolve the conflicts by opening the lines of communication.

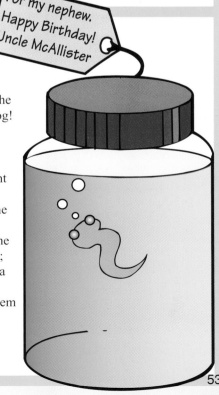

For my nephew. Happy Birthday! Uncle McAllister

The Mysterious Tadpole
Published by The Dial Press

   In *The Mysterious Tadpole*, Louis's Uncle McAllister lives in Scotland, but he always sends Louis the neatest gifts for his birthday. This year Louis received a tadpole. But, as the tadpole grows to enormous proportions, it becomes obvious that he's not turning into a frog!

   Before reading this story, show your students a large gift-wrapped box. Have students brainstorm the identity of its contents. If desired, have students write descriptions of the contents of the box, who and where the gift is from, and what the occasion is for the gift. Read aloud *The Mysterious Tadpole*, and find out if anyone had guessed that the gift might be a tadpole.

   Have students reexamine the last illustration in the book. Discuss with your students the fact that the author leaves us wondering about Uncle McAllister's latest gift. Tape-record each of your youngsters as he privately describes the growth of the hatchling, as well as the problems that this pet creates for Louis's family. Record only two or three stories per tape; then use another tape. Have small groups of students listen to different recordings. When a story is finished, have each group turn off its tape player so that each student has enough time to draw the creature described. When the members of the group are finished, have them compare their drawings, discuss the differences, and replay the story. Have each group repeat this exercise with additional stories as time permits.

contributions by Kathy Curnow, Woolridge Elementary, Midlothian, VA

Best Friends
Published by Dial Books For Young Readers

When he recalls his days as a public school pupil, Kellogg is reminded of teachers who encouraged him to develop his talents and of some wonderful friends. His memories of school and neighborhood relationships are the source of many ideas that eventually filter their way into his books.

Serve chocolate milk to your youngsters before reading aloud *Best Friends*. Afterwards have students discuss their friendships and the positive things that one friend brings to the life of another. Encourage each student to invite one "best" friend from another class to visit your classroom at a specified time. When each friend arrives, have his host introduce him and tell something special about him. Photograph each of your youngsters with his friend. Later attach the photos to a bulletin board titled "The Best Of Friends."

contributions by Carol Bourgeois—Gr. 2, Buena Vista Elementary, Greer, SC

From **PREHISTORIC PINKERTON by Steven Kellogg.** Copyright ©1987 by Steven Kellogg. Used by permission of Dial Books For Young Readers, a division of Penguin Putnam Inc.

Additional Books Written And Illustrated By Steven Kellogg

The Mystery Of The Flying Orange Pumpkin
Published by Dial Books for Young Readers

The Mystery Of The Stolen Blue Paint
Published by Dial Books for Young Readers

The Mystery Of The Missing Red Mitten
Published by Dial Books for Young Readers

The Mystery Of The Magic Green Ball
Published by Dial Books for Young Readers

Ralph's Secret Weapon
Published by Dial Books for Young Readers

Won't Somebody Play With Me?
Published by Dial Books for Young Readers

Additional Books Retold And Illustrated By Steven Kellogg

Paul Bunyan
Published by Morrow Junior Books

Pecos Bill
Published by Morrow Junior Books

Johnny Appleseed
Published by Morrow Junior Books

Mike Fink
Published by Morrow Junior Books

Jack And The Beanstalk
Published by Morrow Junior Books

Eric Kimmel

Noted Storyteller And Award-Winning Author

The words of Eric Kimmel can bring knowledge, laughter, and a love of literature into your classroom! Use the information and the activities that follow to extend your students' enjoyment of this author's work.

by Lisa Leonardi

Meet The Author

Award-winning author Eric A. Kimmel is a prolific teller and writer of stories. Born in Brooklyn, New York, in 1946, Kimmel grew up in a culturally diverse neighborhood where most everyone had a story to tell. Kimmel's grandmother, who moved to the United States from the Western Ukraine, was a wonderful source of stories. Brothers Grimm fairy tales also had a major influence on the young Kimmel. In fact, Kimmel was only in third grade when he began perfecting his storytelling techniques and sharing tales with his classmates.

Kimmel's big break as an author came when he was asked to pen a Hanukkah story. The tale, *Hershel And The Hanukkah Goblins,* earned several awards, including a 1990 Caldecott Honor Book award for illustrator Trina Schart Hyman. After 8 previously published books and 15 years of writing experience, this additional recognition set Kimmel's writing career on a firm course. He has since published more than 20 books—many of which have won awards. Kimmel is perhaps most recognized for his adaptations of folktales from around the world. He is hopeful that children will recognize the basic themes that reappear in the stories and will be encouraged to focus on what unites our world, rather than on what divides it.

Kimmel currently resides in Portland, Oregon, with his wife, a dog, two cats, and several fish. When he's not writing or telling stories, he enjoys a variety of activities that include watching birds, riding motorcycles, baking bread, spinning yarn, knitting sweaters, and riding horses. His latest accomplishment is playing the banjo. Now that's a multitalented writer!

contributions by Peggy A. Sharp

Original Stories

Eric Kimmel's original stories are sure to be enjoyed by your youngsters! Pick and choose from this sampling and the related classroom activities.

Hershel And The Hanukkah Goblins
Illustrated by Trina Schart Hyman
Holiday House, Inc.; 1989
On the first night of Hanukkah, Hershel of Ostropol wanders into a village that—thanks to some Hanukkah-hating goblins—doesn't celebrate Hanukkah. Hershel decides to take matters into his own hands and devises plans to rid the goblins from the village's haunted synagogue. Youngsters will hang onto your every word as Hershel manages to outsmart the grumpy goblins and return the spirit of Hanukkah to the village.

On the fourth, fifth, and sixth nights of Hanukkah, Hershel is visited by other fierce goblins. Hershel fools them all, but the reader is not told how he tricks them. Invite each student to create a goblin using a variety of materials, like construction paper, toilet-paper rolls, wiggle eyes, yarn, and pipe cleaners. Once his goblin is finished, have each student write a clever tactic that Hershel could use to banish this goblin from the synagogue. Students will enjoy sharing their creative goblins and tactics with their classmates.

I Took My Frog To The Library
Illustrated by Blanche Sims
Puffin Books, 1992

When Bridgett visits the library, she brings along her very unusual pets. It's tolerable when Bridgett's frog jumps on the librarian's desk and when the loud laughter of her hyena interrupts storytime. But when her elephant demolishes the library, the librarian strongly suggests that Bridgett leave her pets at home! Like the hyena in the story, your youngsters will laugh out loud at the hilarious animal antics.

Pets are precious, but they can get their owners into some sticky situations! At the conclusion of this story, invite students to describe times when their pets have created problems and explain how they handled the situations. Next have each student write and illustrate a library-related story that features his pet or a pet he'd like to own. Bind the stories into a class book titled "Pet Adventures At The Library." Place the book in the classroom library. For added fun post a sign near the book that prohibits pets from entering your library!

Sharon

One day I took my dog, Hobbes, to my school library. He barked at my friends, chewed on the new library books, and bit the librarian. Hobbes had a great time, but I sure didn't!

One More Original Story
If your students enjoyed *Charlie Drives The Stage*, then it only makes "cents" to follow up with *Four Dollars And Fifty Cents* (Holiday House, Inc.; 1993)—another western tale written by the author!

Charlie Drives The Stage
Illustrated by Glen Rounds
Holiday House, Inc.; 1989
(This book is out of print. Check with your library.)

Senator McCorkle has an important meeting with the president! To board the Washington-bound train, the senator must first travel by stagecoach along a route that is so wrought with dangers that only one driver is willing to take the risk: Charlie Drummond. Not avalanches, robbers, or Indians can outsmart or outrun a stagecoach driven by Charlie. The senator quickly learns that Charlie is full of surprises—but not even the senator is prepared for Charlie's final surprise of the trip!

Senator McCorkle is so impressed with Charlie that he intends to tell the president about him—oops, her! Suggest to students that the senator may have been planning to recommend Charlie for a job. Ask students to recall Charlie's strengths and weaknesses. Keeping these characteristics in mind, have students brainstorm jobs that Charlie could do for the president of the United States. List the students' ideas on the chalkboard. Next ask each youngster to choose a job from the list, then write and illustrate a newspaper article that describes how Charlene helps the president. To publish the students' works, mount the projects on a series of newspaper pages. Decorate the front page of the resulting one-of-a-kind newspaper to show the title "The Grass Valley Times," the date, and a class byline. Laminate the pages for durability; then place the publication in your class library. Extra! Extra! Read all about her!

The Grass Valley TIMES
Mrs. Leonardi's Class
December 11, 1999

DRUMMOND APPOINTED

Drummond Wins Award From The President

Anansi Stories

Eric Kimmel's retellings of Anansi stories are sure to receive rave reviews from your youngsters! Weave a web of amusement with the following stories and activities.

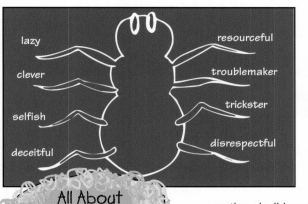

Anansi And The Moss-Covered Rock
Illustrated by Janet Stevens
Holiday House, Inc.; 1988
In this delightful tale of trickery, Anansi the Spider happens upon a strange moss-covered rock that possesses special powers. Anansi realizes he can use the magic of the rock to trick his animal friends. However, Little Bush Deer is onto Anansi's antics and decides to give the trickster a taste of his own medicine!

Anansi is the number-one trickster around! However, it is only Anansi who finds humor in his pranks. Ask students to explain why Anansi's actions are deceitful rather than humorous. To help students analyze Anansi's personality traits, draw the outline of a spider on the chalkboard. Have students brainstorm traits that describe Anansi; then write the traits that are suggested near the ends of the spider's legs.

To extend the activity, have students write sentences describing Anansi's characteristics in rock-shaped booklets. To make a booklet, staple several pages of writing paper between two rock-shaped construction-paper covers. On each booklet page, a student describes a story event that depicts a personality trait of the spider. Then he personalizes and titles the front cover "All About Anansi." If desired have each student glue fabricated moss near the edge of the cover as shown.

Anansi Goes Fishing
Illustrated by Janet Stevens
Holiday House, Inc.; 1992

In this companion tale to Anansi And The Moss-Covered Rock, *lazy Anansi attempts to trick his friend Turtle into catching a fish for him. Unfortunately for Anansi, his plan backfires. Anansi ends up doing all the work and is still left with an empty stomach in the end! Watch this famous trickster get tricked in this comical story that also explains the origin of spider webs.*

The animals that were tricked by Anansi in *Anansi And The Moss-Covered Rock* stand by and watch Anansi get his just rewards in this entertaining sequel. The illustrator has carefully concealed the former Anansi victims behind the river's vegetation. During a second reading, challenge youngsters to locate the animals. Next remind students that both good and bad came from Anansi's failure to trick Turtle. For example, Anansi learns to spin a web; yet he is disgraced in the process. Then encourage students to reflect on Anansi's experiences with this kid-pleasing project. Give each child a 12" x 18" sheet of blue construction paper and eight small fish cutouts: four yellow and four orange. On each yellow fish, a student writes a positive event that Anansi experienced. On each orange fish, he writes a negative event that the spider experienced. Next the student illustrates Anansi and a fishing net on his blue paper; then he glues his fish cutouts around the net as shown.

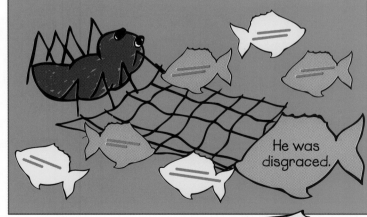

He was disgraced.

He learned to spin a web.

Another Anansi Tale
If your students enjoyed the first two Anansi retellings by Eric Kimmel,
they're sure to love *Anansi And The Talking Melon* (Holiday House, Inc.; 1995).
And who knows? The author could be cooking up yet another Anansi tale!

Folktales From Other Countries

The following featured books are just a sampling of the author's retellings of folktales from around the world. Use the provided activities to complement these enjoyable stories.

Baba Yaga: A Russian Folktale
Illustrated by Megan Lloyd
Holiday House, Inc.; 1993

One afternoon Marina's evil stepmother sends her to visit Auntie-in-the-Forest, who is known to all as Baba Yaga, *a very mean and conniving witch. Shaking with fear, Marina sets out to face her unquestionable doom. Along the way she kindly accepts the advice of a friendly frog. Will the frog's advice be enough to save Marina from Baba Yaga?*

At the conclusion of this folktale, emphasize that—just like in the fairy tale *Cinderella*—inner beauty prevails over evil. Ask students to state similarities and differences between Marina and Cinderella, and write their responses on the chalkboard. Then have each student refer to the posted information as she completes a copy of page 59. Conclude this activity by taking a class poll to determine which of these two characters your students like best.

The Greatest Of All: A Japanese Folktale
Illustrated by Giora Carmi
Holiday House, Inc.; 1995

In this lighthearted Japanese tale, Father Mouse searches for the greatest husband for his daughter. In his search he approaches the emperor, the sun, a cloud, the wind, and a wall before he finds a very unexpected—yet very suitable—suitor.

After reading the story aloud, write a student-generated list of story events on the chalkboard. Then divide the class into groups of eight students each. Ask each group member to illustrate a different story character on provided paper, then cut out and glue the character to a craft stick. Invite each group to use its puppets to reenact Father Mouse's search for the mightiest husband. Or challenge each group to create another set of possible suitors for a telling of a similar story. There's no doubt that the greatest of all theatrics will be performed by your students!

An Additional Folktale
Your students are sure to be touched by Eric Kimmel's adapted tale *Sirko And The Wolf: A Ukrainian Tale* (Holiday House, Inc.; 1997). This heartwarming story explains the bond that dogs and wolves share.

Two Kind Characters

Think about the two characters shown.

Write words that describe only Marina in her bucket.
Write words that describe only Cinderella in her bucket.

Write words that describe both
Marina and Cinderella in the puddle.

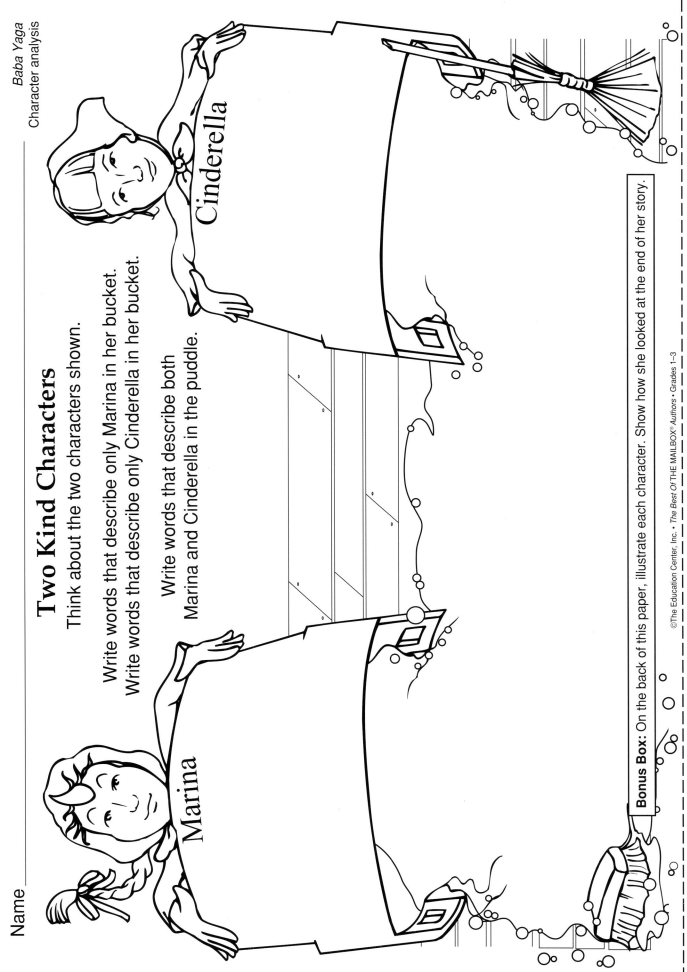

Cinderella

Marina

Bonus Box: On the back of this paper, illustrate each character. Show how she looked at the end of her story.

©The Education Center, Inc. • *The Best Of THE MAILBOX® Authors* • Grades 1–3

Note To Teacher: Use with *Baba Yaga: A Russian Folktale* on page 58.

Virginia Kroll
Author Extraordinaire

Virginia Kroll has won the hearts of numerous children, teachers, and adults by sharing her gift of writing. The following pages feature only a few of her outstanding books, but that's not a concern. As Ms. Kroll's fans know—it only takes one!

by Donna C. Kester Phillips

About The Author

As a former elementary school teacher, a mother of six children ranging in ages from eight to 26, a grandmother, and an author of over 22 children's books—Virginia Kroll understands children! A recreational writer of poetry and greeting cards, Virginia first tried her hand at writing articles and short stories for publication in 1984. It wasn't until five years later that she ventured into writing children's books.

Virginia's books are based on her experiences and those of her family and friends. But Virginia says that she draws her insight and guidance from what she calls her "word angels." These visions are what allow her to use her writing as an instrument to achieve her mission in life. Virginia's mission, she says, is to change lives. Through her work she hopes to show children how much the people of the world are alike—bridging the cultural differences that are present in what Virginia calls our "global village."

Virginia reads to her children each morning as they eat their breakfast. This, she believes, is the most important thing that she can do for her children. Her love of children and animals (she has 29 pets with more guinea pigs on the way!) are the center of her work. In Virginia's own words, "My greatest reward is receiving letters from the children who read my books." These letters let her know that her books really do help to change lives.

Masai And I

Illustrated by Nancy Carpenter
Four Winds Press, 1992

In Masai And I, *Virginia Kroll tells the story of what it might be like to be a child of the Masai people of Africa. As the young girl goes through her day, she imagines what she would be doing if she lived with the Masai. Through this comparison of daily activities, youngsters learn that people are much the same, even though lifestyles and cultures greatly differ. The author believes this to be her best book to date.*

This account provides a wonderful link to community and/or cultural studies. Challenge each student to imagine what life would be like if he had been born in another country or culture. Then have students create a class big book or individual booklets using the format shown below. After the booklet pages have been illustrated, compile them between student-decorated covers. If a class big book results, invite neighboring classes to your room for an oral presentation of the story. If the product is individual booklets, set aside time for students to share their work with their classmates.

If I were _____, my house would be…
If I were _____, I would get my water and food…
If I were _____ and I wanted dessert, I would…
If I were _____, at night I would…
If I were _____, I would go to bed…
If I were _____, my pets would be…
If I were _____, I would wear…
If I were _____ and going to a party, I would…
If I were _____, I would travel by…
If I were _____, I would love and respect my…
If I were _____, my name might be…

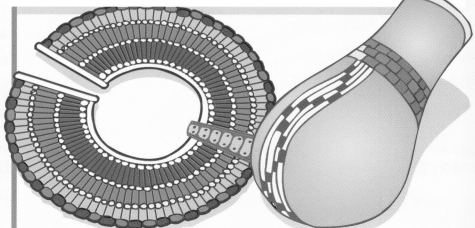

Pink Paper Swans

Illustrated by Nancy L. Clouse
William B. Eerdmans Publishing Company, 1994
Janetta, intrigued by the paper animals that her neighbor Mrs. Tsujimoto makes, learns the art of origami and becomes Mrs. Tsujimoto's hands when her arthritis makes it difficult for her to continue.

Virginia Kroll's favorite place to visit as a child was a Japanese store where Mrs. Tsujimoto taught the art of origami. Although Virginia was fascinated by the paper folding and worked hard to master it, she never did. So she decided to write a story about a child who was successful! There's little doubt that your students will be eager to try their hands at origami. Although directions for making a paper swan are included at the end of the book, you may want to choose simpler projects for your beginning paper folders. There are many good books that provide directions for folding frogs, fish, cats, giraffes, crabs, birds, and scores of other creatures. To display the students' origami projects, cover the lower half of a bulletin board with green paper and the upper half with blue paper. Enlist your students' help in creating appropriate habitats for their folded critters. Then, using straight pins, display the projects in the appropriate environments. Now that's impressive!

Sweet Magnolia

Illustrated by Laura Jacques
Charlesbridge Publishing, 1995
The author's sister was the inspiration for this story that takes place in the bayous of Louisiana. When six-year-old Denise visits her grandmother, a wildlife rehabilitator, she helps heal and free an injured baby bird. Sprinkled with images and words of Cajun and Creole culture, this book will enlighten and enrich the lives of the children who experience it.

The rich illustrations and the poetic language of this sweet story are a treat for the eyes and ears. These elements set the stage for children to investigate the wild animals of the bayou and learn about these animals' special needs. Start by having the children generate a list of the animals that are named or illustrated in the story. Then have each child choose an animal from the list that she would like to have for a pet and illustrate it on the top half of a sheet of drawing paper. Next have each child fold and unfold a second sheet of paper to create two columns. In the left column, she lists reasons why she would like to have the animal she illustrated. In the right column, she lists reasons why it would be unfair to make this animal her pet. Conclude the activity by asking each youngster to illustrate a domesticated animal that is somewhat similar to the wild animal, but that would make a good pet.

Set aside time for students to share their work with their classmates. This activity will enrich the children's book experience and do justice to the intent of the author—which is understanding the importance of respecting animals in the wild.

Jaha And Jamil
Went Down The Hill:
An African Mother Goose

Illustrated by Katherine Roundtree
Charlesbridge Publishing, 1995
Through her poetry Virginia Kroll introduces children to African customs, traditions, and cultures. Each page of rhymes and illustrations represents a different African country and is referenced by a map at the end of the book.

Thanks to Virginia, the fun and learning never stop in this book. From the rhythm of the rhymes to the knowledge gained about Africa and its people, this book will make a difference in the lives of your children. To make the most of this experience, enlarge and display a map of Africa like the one shown at the back of the book. Laminate a sheet of poster board and display it next to the map. Use one pushpin to attach one end of a yarn length near the blank poster. Insert a second pushpin nearby. Every few days copy a different poem from the book onto the blank poster and use the extra pushpin to secure the unattached yarn end to the appropriate African country. Encourage students to practice reading the rhyme. Also challenge them to recall the original Mother Goose rhyme on which it is based. If desired, instruct students to copy each posted rhyme for handwriting practice. Have each student keep his handwriting papers in a personalized folder. When appropriate each student can illustrate his papers and compile them between a self-decorated construction-paper cover.

Hats Off To Hair!

Illustrated by Kay Life
Charlesbridge Publishing, 1995
It's a celebration of hair! How many ways can it be cut, combed, or colored? Virginia Kroll has a pretty good idea! Through the rhythm and rhyme of her words, readers discover a lot about hairdos. In the process vocabularies are enriched and a greater understanding of celebrating differences is achieved.

Who hasn't at some point in his or her life longed for someone else's hair? For a fun follow-up activity to this delightful romp, give each child a piece of tagboard in which you have cut a circle large enough to reveal a child's face. Then—using yarn, felt, ribbon, markers, crayons, or any other desired medium—have each child create a new "do." Ask students to name their new hairdos, too. Students may wish to refer to the glossary of hairdo terminology at the back of the book for inspiration. When the projects are finished, set aside time for students to take turns modeling the different do's for their classmates. If a large mirror is available, tape several of the projects to the mirror. Students can take turns looking into the mirror and seeing themselves sporting a variety of original hairdos!

Writing To The Author

Virginia Kroll would love to hear from your students. She prefers class letters and she asks that the letters be sent to her in care of the publisher of the book about which you are corresponding. The address of the publisher is listed inside the book—either at the front or the back.

Leo Lionni
Author And Illustrator

This collection of classroom-tested ideas features follow-up activities for many of Leo Lionni's books.

Leo Lionni knew at an early age that he wanted to become an artist. A native of Holland, Lionni spent much of his childhood in art museums in Amsterdam teaching himself to draw. He came to the United States in 1939 as an established painter and was soon recognized as a "dynamic talent in commercial design." Quite a feat for a fellow without any formal art training!

Lionni's career as an author and illustrator of children's books began by chance in the late 1950s. While traveling by train with his grandchildren, he created an entertaining story to pass the time. Later he worked the material into a book. The book, *Little Blue And Little Yellow,* has since become a classic in children's literature.

With his deep concern for quality and his belief that good children's books should appeal to all those who savor the childlike wonder and joy of life, Leo Lionni's international acclaim comes as no surprise.

Wishing On A Purple Stone

In *Alexander And The Wind-Up Mouse,* a purple stone has magical powers. After reading the story aloud to your youngsters, instruct each student to tear a pebble shape from a piece of purple construction paper. Have the student mount his pebble onto a 9" x 12" sheet of art paper, then copy and complete the following sentence: "If I had a magic purple pebble, I would wish for...." After the students have illustrated their wishes, invite the youngsters to share their projects with their classmates.

Christine Joyner—Gr. 1
Lincoln Heights GT
    Magnet
Fuquay-Varina, NC

What Will I Be?

Matthew's Dream is a wonderful story for exploring your youngsters' personal aspirations. After reading the book aloud to your class, invite students to share their dreams for the future. Find out how your students think their personal experiences have influenced their dreams. Then discuss how Matthew decided that he wanted to become a painter. Together reexamine the illustrations in the book. For a fun follow-up, provide bold colors of paint and art paper for students to create their own original masterpieces. As the youngsters paint, play classical background music. Encourage students to title and sign their works of art; then display the masterpieces in a well-traveled area such as a school hallway.

Melissa Beasley—Chapter I, North Columbia Elementary, Appling, GA

Discussing Communities

Several of Leo Lionni's mice tales—such as *Tillie And The Wall, Frederick,* and *Mr. McMouse*—make excellent springboards for community-related discussions. Have students compare each mouse community to their own community. Emphasize the importance of community members working together to achieve common goals. Also clarify how an individual's efforts can influence his or her community. Finally brainstorm ways the class could contribute to its community; then make plans to put the students' ideas into action!

Angela Fiorillo—Gr. 2
Hillside Grade School
New Hyde Park, NY

animals	foods	people
cows	corn	farmers
horses	nuts	
	wheat	

Give A Mouse A Home

For a perfect follow-up to *Frederick,* have each youngster mold a portion of clay or dough into a mouse shape. When the shapes have thoroughly dried and hardened, have students paint their mice as desired. Ask students to recall from the story how Frederick and the members of his family prepared for winter. Then have each student ponder the perfect winter home for his painted pal. Ask students to consider where their mice should live, whom they should live with, and what supplies their mice will need. Then challenge each child to create a winter home for his mouse. If desired, provide a class supply of empty shoeboxes for this activity. Display the completed projects in the school media center.

Raquel Brogan—Special Education Grs. K-2
Washington School
North Arlington, NJ

Winter Preparations

Follow up a first reading of *Frederick* by drawing a chart like the one shown. Under your students' direction, list the different *animals, foods,* and *people* mentioned in the story. When the students have exhausted their memories, reread the story a second time. Students can verify the items listed and note those that were overlooked. Complete the chart at the conclusion of the second reading; then discuss what effects these animals, foods, and people had on this mouse family's winter preparations.

Carrie Winkelman—Grs. 3-4 MH: Mild
Harrison Elementary
Omaha, NE

Mice With Character

Students are sure to enjoy trying their hand at creating mouse-related illustrations that resemble Lionni originals. As a class carefully examine several Lionni illustrations that feature mice. Then provide construction paper in assorted colors, fine-tip markers, glue, scissors, and a student supply of 9" x 12" sheets of white construction paper. Have students tear, snip, and glue construction-paper shapes onto their white paper to create Lionni-like illustrations. Display the completed projects on a bulletin board entitled "Just Like Lionni!"

Marian Johnson—Grs. 1-2, Roosevelt Elementary, McPherson, KS

Fishy Booklets

After you finish an oral reading of *Swimmy,* get students in the swim of things with this booklet project. To make her booklet, a student traces a fish shape onto two sheets of red construction paper and three sheets of white paper. Next she staples the white pages between the colored pages and attaches a fish eye (a tiny dark-colored fish cutout) to the front cover of her resulting booklet. Engage students in a class discussion about the beginning, the middle, and the ending of *Swimmy;* then have each student summarize and illustrate the three story parts on the appropriate pages in her booklet.

Connie Moffeit—Gr. 2, Western Oaks Elementary, Bethany, OK

An "Eggs-traordinary" Tale

An Extraordinary Egg (Alfred A. Knopf, 1994) is a fable about friendship with a touch of mistaken identity. The hatching of a beautiful egg delights three froggie friends. The newborn "chicken" is quickly accepted into the frogs' friendship circle and from sunup to sundown, a good time is had by all. When at last the so-called chicken is reunited with her mother, the frogs find it amusing that the mother calls her child her "sweet little alligator." Ask students why they think the foursome from the story formed a friendship so easily. Also ask students why they think some friendships are formed more easily than others. Then find out what kinds of qualities your students look for in their friends.

The booklet project on page 66 is a fun culminating activity. Duplicate student copies of the booklet on white construction paper. To make a booklet, a student reads and illustrates each sentence; then he numbers the pages in the order that the events happened in the story. After completing the booklet cover, he cuts on the dotted lines, sequentially stacks the pages, and staples his booklet together. Or have each student use the provided cover as a title page. To create egg-shaped covers, have each youngster stack, trim, and decorate two 3 1/2" x 5" sheets of construction paper.

In The Swim

Expect squeals of delight from your youngsters when they view the final results of this follow-up activity to *Swimmy.* Using strawberry- or cherry-flavored Jell-O® and the directions on the back of the gelatin box, prepare a batch of Jell-O® Jigglers™. When the gelatin has set, have each student use a fish-shaped cookie cutter to cut out a fish shape. Arrange the gelatin cutouts on a large tray in the shape of a fish. Insert a fish eye—a dark-colored, fish-shaped cracker or cookie—and the creation is complete. Take a few moments to admire the fishy creation with your students; then let the eating begin!

Andrea M. Troisi—Librarian
LaSalle Middle School
Niagara Falls, NY

From AN EXTRA-ORDINARY EGG by Leo Lionni Copyright © 1994 by Leo Lionni. Reprinted by permission of Alfred A. Knopf, Inc.

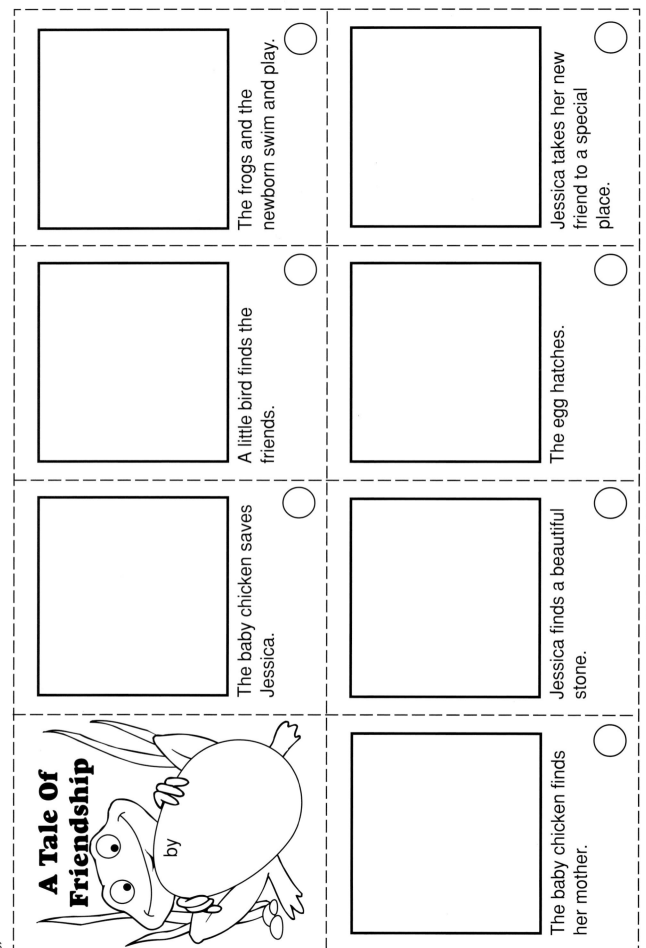

The frogs and the newborn swim and play. ◯

Jessica takes her new friend to a special place. ◯

A little bird finds the friends. ◯

The egg hatches. ◯

The baby chicken saves Jessica. ◯

Jessica finds a beautiful stone. ◯

A Tale Of Friendship

by

The baby chicken finds her mother. ◯

©The Education Center, Inc. • *The Best Of* THE MAILBOX® *Authors* • Grades 1–3 • Key p. 98

Note To Teacher: Use with "An 'Eggs-traordinary' Tale" on page 65.

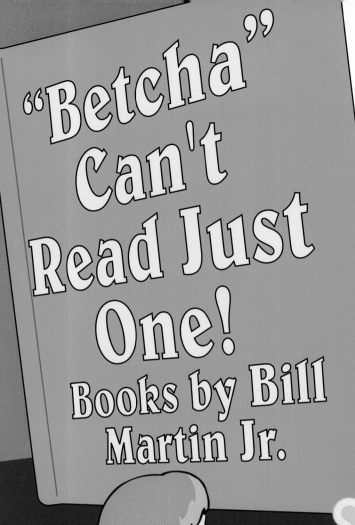

"Betcha" Can't Read Just One!

Books by Bill Martin Jr.

Bill Martin Jr.'s infectious writing style keeps readers coming back for book after book after book. Use this sampling of Bill Martin books and the related activities to nurture your students' love of reading.

by Anne Bustard

William Who?

Known to most folks as Bill Martin Jr., William Ivan Martin began writing children's books more than 50 years ago. To date he has published well over 100 different titles. That's pretty amazing for a young Kansas boy who struggled to learn to read. Despite Martin's poor reading ability, he managed to proceed through school with a love of books. He credits his storytelling grandmother, his fifth-grade teacher who read aloud to the class twice a day, and his high school drama teacher for instilling in him a love of books, an interest in language, and a desire to read. Martin read his first book—from start to finish—during his freshman year of college. He recalls the experience as "a laborious but glorious undertaking."

Martin's knowledge and passion for books have empowered him to pursue many reading-related careers that include being a teacher, a principal, an editor, a children's textbook creator, a video producer, a lecturer, and a storyteller. As an advocate for reading and teachers, Martin believes in giving children reading experiences that provide ample opportunities for success.

In March 1999, Bill Martin Jr. celebrated his 83rd birthday. He resides in Texas and continues to be active in the publishing world.

Brown Bear, Brown Bear, What Do You See?

Written by Bill Martin Jr. & Illustrated by Eric Carle
Henry Holt And Company, Inc.; 1992
A parade of colorful critters traipses across the pages of this most beloved book. The author's engaging and predictable text is magnified by the illustrator's large, colorful collages. What results is an unspoken invitation for listeners to join in on the fun!

After a few oral readings of the book, introduce students to this large-group predictable-pattern game. Sit with your students on the floor in a large circle formation. To play the game, instruct students to repeat the question "Teacher, Teacher, what do you see?" when you touch your ear. Touch your ear; then respond to your students' question as follows: "I see [name of student to your right] wearing [appropriate color word] to the right of me." To continue the game, the student to your right touches her ear. The class asks the original question, substituting the child's name for *Teacher*. The student answers her classmates' question using the established pattern. Continue playing the game in this manner. When each child has taken her turn, conclude the game in a manner that imitates the book's conclusion.

blue
yellow
green
white

wingingly
slowly
knowingly
dizzily
wildly
trrrr-r-r-r-ippingly

The Maestro Plays

Written by Bill Martin Jr. & Illustrated by Vladimir Radunsky
Harcourt Brace & Company, 1996
How does the maestro play? "Singingly," "ringingly," and "wingingly" name a few of the ways! In this book adverbs take center stage as a master of music plays assorted instruments. Dynamic illustrations accompany the action-packed performance. And when the concert is over, claps and bravos fill the pages. Encore! Encore!

Set the stage for the maestro's high-energy recital by introducing students to a variety of instruments and the sounds that they make. Recruit your school's music teacher (or bandleader) to help you with this project. Members of your students' families may also be able to help. When you read the book aloud, alter the tempo and volume of your voice to match those which are conveyed on the book's pages. During a second reading, take time to identify the instruments that are being played and the maestro's talents. Also help students conclude that this *maestro* is a master of music. Then, as an encore, take your students to an unobstructed area like the school gym and read the book a third time. Invite students to *feel* the music from their heads to their toes!

Chicka Chicka Boom Boom

Written by Bill Martin Jr. and John Archambault
Illustrated by Lois Ehlert
Simon And Schuster Books For Young Readers, 1989
In this rollicking rhyme the letters of the alphabet race each other up a coconut tree. Then all too quickly, the tree gives away and the letters come tumbling down—Chicka chicka…BOOM! BOOM! Pretty polka-dotted borders trim pages of bright, bold letters—making this lively story bounce even higher!

Double the fun by having students contribute to a colorful display as they act out this lively rhyme. In advance, cover a bulletin board with dark blue paper. Mount a large coconut tree cutout, a paper moon, and the title "Chicka Chicka Boom Boom!" on the paper-covered board. Next have each child cut out and decorate a different alphabet letter. During an oral reading of the story, each child stands and displays her artwork when her letter is mentioned. When all the letters tumble from the tree, the students chant, "Chicka chicka boom boom!" and drop to the floor. Then, as the letters dust themselves off and get arranged alphabetically, have the students do the same—right by your classroom coconut tree. At the conclusion of the story, mount the student-created letters on the display. Hey! Where's that *a* going?

The Wild West

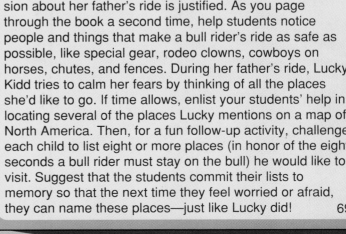

Barn Dance!

Written by Bill Martin Jr. and John Archambault
Illustrated by Ted Rand
Henry Holt And Company, Inc.; 1986
Here's a toe-tappin', knee-slappin', do-si-doin' fantasy! Summoned by an owl, a young pajama-clad boy slips outside on a moonlit night. The faint sounds of music lead the wide-eyed lad to a most unusual barn dance. Written in rhyme, this high-spirited page-turner gives readers the inside scoop on what farm animals do when their caretakers are sound asleep!

What could be more fun than having your own toe-tappin' hoedown? Plan to play some square-dance music, and if possible enlist the P.E. teacher or a parent volunteer to teach your youngsters a few simple square-dance steps. If dancing is out of the question, make plans to play a game of Scarecrow Says. After all, the fiddle-playing scarecrow does play a significant role in this story. To play this harvest version of Simon Says, students follow only the directions prefaced by "Scarecrow says." Students who miss form a circle around the remaining players and clap their hands to the music. Finish the game by having the circle of students join hands and skip to the right and to the left around the remaining players.

White Dynamite And Curly Kidd

Written by Bill Martin Jr. and John Archambault
Illustrated by Ted Rand
Henry Holt And Company, Inc.; 1986
Ride 'em, Cowboy! Hold on tight as Curly Kidd rides the fiercest bull on the rodeo circuit—appropriately named White Dynamite. Curly's youngster, Lucky Kidd, anxiously watches Curly prepare for and participate in the event—all the while dreaming of one day becoming a bull rider too. Written entirely in dialogue, this western-flavored story and its surprise ending are sure to stir up some excitement in your classroom!

Bull riding is a dangerous sport and Lucky's apprehension about her father's ride is justified. As you page through the book a second time, help students notice people and things that make a bull rider's ride as safe as possible, like special gear, rodeo clowns, cowboys on horses, chutes, and fences. During her father's ride, Lucky Kidd tries to calm her fears by thinking of all the places she'd like to go. If time allows, enlist your students' help in locating several of the places Lucky mentions on a map of North America. Then, for a fun follow-up activity, challenge each child to list eight or more places (in honor of the eight seconds a bull rider must stay on the bull) he would like to visit. Suggest that the students commit their lists to memory so that the next time they feel worried or afraid, they can name these places—just like Lucky did!

Knots On A Counting Rope

Written by Bill Martin Jr. and John Archambault
Illustrated by Ted Rand
Henry Holt And Company, Inc.; 1987

In this touching tale a grandfather promises his grandson, Boy-Strength-Of-Blue-Horses, that his love will always surround the boy. As the older man reminisces about the boy's life, the boy—who is blind—is reminded once again of the importance of seeing with his heart.

At the conclusion of this story, ask students to reflect on the relationship that the grandfather and the boy share. Encourage students to name the different ways that the grandfather has influenced the young boy's life. Next find out what childhood stories are important to your students. Ask each student to talk with a family member about a favorite childhood story. If desired, give each child a one-foot length of twine. Instruct the students to add a knot to the rope each time they discuss their stories with their family members. Then, on a designated day, set aside time for interested students to orally share their stories with their classmates.

The Willies

Old Devil Wind

Written by Bill Martin Jr. & Illustrated by Barry Root
Harcourt Brace & Company, 1993

Picture an old creaky house on a dark and stormy night, and you've captured the setting of this dramatic cumulative tale. The rickety mansion slowly comes to life as one object after another joins in making ghostly noises. But when the wind takes its turn, the unsuspecting objects are scattered every which way! Barry Root's dark and moody illustrations perfectly suit the climactic nature of this delightfully eerie escapade.

This story screams out for reader participation! Using the provided chart, write each object and its corresponding sounds on a card. After an initial oral reading of the story, divide the class into ten groups and give each group a programmed card. Provide time for the groups to rehearse their sound effects. Then, during a second oral reading, pause after each object has declared its sound and wait for the appropriate group to provide the sound effect. Ask the entire class to contribute to the wind's ghostly noise. If desired, also pause after each object has been blown away so that the appropriate group can repeat its sound effect. For added fun, redistribute the sound cards to different groups and read the story again—and again and again!

Object	Sound Effect
ghost	"wail, wail, wail, wail"
stool	"thump, thump, thump, thump"
broom	"swish, swish, swish, swish"
candle	"flicker, flicker, flicker, flicker"
fire	"smoke, smoke, smoke, smoke"
window	"rattle, rattle, rattle, rattle"
floor	"creak, creak, creak, creak"
door	"slam, slam, slam, slam"
owl	"hoot, hoot, hoot, hoot"
witch	"fly, fly, fly, fly"

Candle
"flicker, flicker, flicker, flicker"

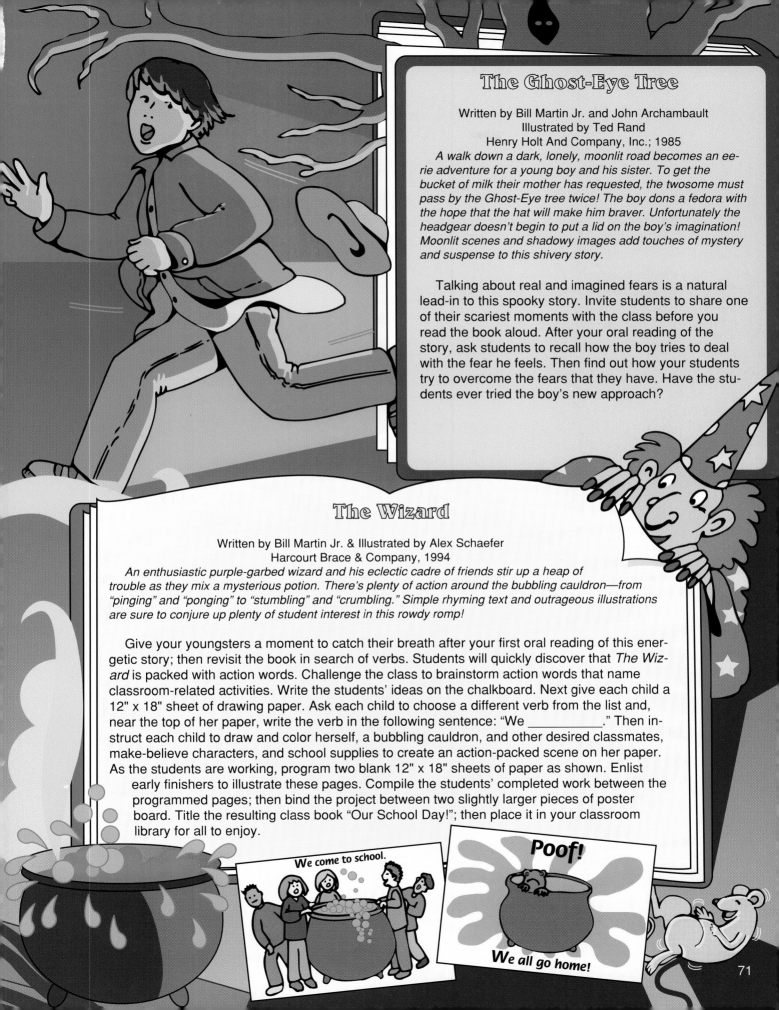

The Ghost-Eye Tree

Written by Bill Martin Jr. and John Archambault
Illustrated by Ted Rand
Henry Holt And Company, Inc.; 1985

A walk down a dark, lonely, moonlit road becomes an eerie adventure for a young boy and his sister. To get the bucket of milk their mother has requested, the twosome must pass by the Ghost-Eye tree twice! The boy dons a fedora with the hope that the hat will make him braver. Unfortunately the headgear doesn't begin to put a lid on the boy's imagination! Moonlit scenes and shadowy images add touches of mystery and suspense to this shivery story.

Talking about real and imagined fears is a natural lead-in to this spooky story. Invite students to share one of their scariest moments with the class before you read the book aloud. After your oral reading of the story, ask students to recall how the boy tries to deal with the fear he feels. Then find out how your students try to overcome the fears that they have. Have the students ever tried the boy's new approach?

The Wizard

Written by Bill Martin Jr. & Illustrated by Alex Schaefer
Harcourt Brace & Company, 1994

An enthusiastic purple-garbed wizard and his eclectic cadre of friends stir up a heap of trouble as they mix a mysterious potion. There's plenty of action around the bubbling cauldron—from "pinging" and "ponging" to "stumbling" and "crumbling." Simple rhyming text and outrageous illustrations are sure to conjure up plenty of student interest in this rowdy romp!

Give your youngsters a moment to catch their breath after your first oral reading of this energetic story; then revisit the book in search of verbs. Students will quickly discover that *The Wizard* is packed with action words. Challenge the class to brainstorm action words that name classroom-related activities. Write the students' ideas on the chalkboard. Next give each child a 12" x 18" sheet of drawing paper. Ask each child to choose a different verb from the list and, near the top of her paper, write the verb in the following sentence: "We _____." Then instruct each child to draw and color herself, a bubbling cauldron, and other desired classmates, make-believe characters, and school supplies to create an action-packed scene on her paper. As the students are working, program two blank 12" x 18" sheets of paper as shown. Enlist early finishers to illustrate these pages. Compile the students' completed work between the programmed pages; then bind the project between two slightly larger pieces of poster board. Title the resulting class book "Our School Day!"; then place it in your classroom library for all to enjoy.

We come to school.

Poof!

We all go home!

Gerald McDermott

A Master Of Storytelling And Illustration

About The Author

Gerald McDermott is an internationally known author and illustrator who has created numerous books and animated films for children. A master of his craft, McDermott can spin and illustrate tales that represent the cultures of many peoples.

McDermott's career began at the young age of four when his parents enrolled him in art school. Until the age of 14, he attended classes at the Detroit Institute Of Art every Saturday morning. In the afternoons he explored the galleries. By the age of nine, McDermott knew he was destined to become an artist.

McDermott's innovative picture books have earned him several prestigious awards including the Caldecott Medal for *Arrow To The Sun: A Pueblo Indian Tale,* and Caldecott Honors for *Anansi The Spider: A Tale From The Ashanti* and *Raven: A Trickster Tale From The Pacific Northwest.* In addition to writing and illustrating, McDermott is Primary Education Program Director for the Joseph Campbell Foundation on mythology in education. A native of Detroit, Michigan, the author currently resides in southern California.

Pick and choose from this sampling of McDermott's work and the related classroom activities.

Anansi The Spider: A Tale From The Ashanti

Anansi's six sons save their father from a terrible fate. Unable to decide which one son should be rewarded, Anansi enlists the help of Nyame—The God Of All Things.

No doubt each of your youngsters will have an opinion about which son should receive the prize Anansi has found. Draw a graph on the chalkboard that lists the names of the six sons. In turn have each child express and defend his opinion, then color the corresponding space on the class graph. After students have interpreted the completed graph, use the graph to create an assortment of problem-solving activities.

Arlene Levine—Gr. 1, Freeman School, Phillipsburg, NJ

These moon-shaped journals are the perfect places for students to write additional tales about Anansi and his six sons. To make a journal, staple several blank, circular pages between two slightly larger yellow construction-paper covers. Students can write and illustrate a series of spider-related tales. Or they can write and illustrate stories that explain which son becomes the keeper of the moon.

Arlene Levine—Gr. 1

Stories of Anansi by Nikki Stamnos

Arrow To The Sun: A Pueblo Indian Tale

This adaptation of a Pueblo tale won the Caldecott Medal in 1975. Bright, bold graphics and few words tell the tale of how the spirit of the sun was brought down to the Pueblo people.

Once at the sun, the Boy is challenged by four *kivas* (ceremonial chambers). Have students reexamine these illustrations and describe the inhabitants of each chamber as the Boy enters and as he exits. The Boy tames the lions, serpents, and bees instead of killing them. Ask your youngsters to propose ways to tame the inhabitants of kivas filled with bears, spiders, and crocodiles.

This book is a vivid visual reminder of the Indian reverence for the source of all life: the Solar Fire. Students—inspired by McDermott's bold illustrations—can produce bright paper-plate sunbursts of their own. To make a sun, sketch a desired design on a paper plate. Then use crayons, markers, or tempera paints to give color to your sun.

The Stonecutter: A Japanese Folk Tale

A foolish longing for power forever changes the life of a lowly stonecutter. This ancient Japanese fable is a tale of wishes and dreams—and consequences.

Tasaku's continuous quest for more and more power becomes his ultimate undoing. Invite your students to talk about their wishes and dreams. Find out what they learned from Tasaku's experience and how they can apply this new knowledge to their pursuit of happiness. Next have each child copy, complete, and illustrate the following: "Happiness is…." Showcase the completed projects on a bulletin board featuring a large, mountain-shaped cutout and the title "Happiness Is…." Or bind them into a book bearing a similar cover.

Papagayo: The Mischief Maker

The noisy daytime habits of a mischievous parrot perturb the nocturnal creatures of the rain forest. But the nocturnal bunch has a change of heart when Papagayo's noisy ways save the day!

You won't hear many squawks of protest when you unveil this follow-up art activity! In advance cover a bulletin board with bright blue paper. Attach a white moon-shaped cutout and the title "Papagayo's Rain Forest." As a class, admire the author's bright, bold, and colorful rain-forest artwork. Then challenge your students to create a similar scene. To do this, divide the class into small groups and assign each group a portion of the rain forest. For example, different groups could be responsible for the rain-forest vegetation, the nocturnal creatures, Papagayo, and the moon-dog. Each group uses bright, bold tempera paints or markers to illustrate its assigned topic on white art paper. Then each group cuts out its artwork and attaches it to the display. Wow! Wouldn't Mr. McDermott be impressed?

Lisa Kelley—Gr. 1, James Walker Elementary, Blue Springs, MO

Daniel O'Rourke: An Irish Tale

Hold on tight! This fast-paced and lighthearted fantasy about a young Irishman may sweep you off your feet—and that's no blarney!

Daniel O'Rourke's ordeal creates a perfect setting for a bit of St. Patrick's Day creative writing. Discuss Daniel's adventures with your youngsters. Have students explain how each one related to a previous incident in Daniel's life. Challenge students to carry out this theme as they write and illustrate additional adventures for this likable Irishman. Be sure to set aside time for interested students to share their Irish tales. If desired bind the stories between booklet covers cut in the shape of an island. Title the book "Daniel O'Rourke's Island Adventures."

Fran Palffy, Parma Park Christian Life Academy, Parma, OH

It looks like green cheese, but does it taste like it? Students are sure to enjoy this green cheese look-alike!

Green Cheese Delight

3-oz. package lime gelatin
1 cup boiling water
1 cup cold water

24-oz. container of cottage cheese
12-oz. container of thawed Cool Whip®
1 cup miniature marshmallows

In a large bowl, use the water to prepare the lime gelatin according to the package directions. Refrigerate the gelatin until it begins to thicken. In a second bowl, mix together the cottage cheese, the Cool Whip®, and the marshmallows. Fold this mixture into the thickened gelatin. Refrigerate until set. Makes approximately 25 to 30 small servings.

Fran Palffy

Step 1   Step 2

Tim O'Toole And The Wee Folk: An Irish Tale

Penniless Tim O'Toole teams up with the wee folk to trick the McGoons into giving him back his fortune.

The luck of the Irish was with Tim O'Toole when he spied the wee folk in the light of day. But because Tim couldn't keep from boasting, his good fortune quickly turned into misfortune—more than once! Ask your youngsters how they feel about boasting. When do they think boasting is acceptable? not acceptable? What did they learn from Tim O'Toole's experience?

When your students make a troop of wee folk, the luck of the Irish is sure to find its way into your classroom!

For each leprechaun you will need:

— three 3" green construction-paper squares (body)
— a 2" x 3" green construction-paper strip (hat)
— two 2" black paper squares (boots)
— two 2" skin-tone construction-paper squares (hands)
— one 2 1/2" skin-tone construction-paper circle
— scraps of black and yellow construction paper
— a fine-tip marker
— yarn for the beard
— scissors
— glue

Directions:

1. Cut a heart shape from each green square. To form the body, glue the points of the heart shapes together as shown.
2. Use the marker to draw a face on the skin-tone circle. Glue the resulting face in place.
3. Trim the green rectangle into a hat shape. Glue the hat in place.
4. Stack the skin-tone squares. Cut out two matching hand shapes. Glue the hands in place.
5. Stack the black squares. Cut out two matching boot shapes. Glue the boots in place.
6. Cut a hat band and a hat buckle, a belt and a belt buckle, and two shoe buckles from paper scraps. Glue the cutouts in place.
7. Glue a yarn beard in place.

Zomo The Rabbit: A Trickster Tale From West Africa

Zomo the Rabbit isn't very big and he isn't very strong—but he's quite clever! Now he also wants to be wise. Can Zomo prove to the Sky God that he's worthy of wisdom?

At the end of the story, Sky God warns Zomo about his shortcomings. Ask students to recall why Zomo stole from Big Fish, Wild Cow, and Leopard. Then ask the youngsters to explain why they do or do not think Zomo demonstrated true wisdom. Next divide the class into groups of five students each. Have each group member illustrate a different story character, then cut out and glue his character to a craft stick. Invite each group to use their puppets to reenact Zomo's story or to create a new adventure for Zomo, Sky God, Big Fish, Wild Cow, and Leopard.

Raven: A Trickster Tale From The Pacific Northwest

When Raven came to the world, it was in total darkness. Can the wise and clever Raven find the gift of light, and then give it to the world?

Raven felt sorry for the people who were living in the cold darkness, so he took it upon himself to find light for the world. Ask students to brainstorm things that trouble them—things in the world that they wish they could change. List the students' ideas on the chalkboard. Ask each child to choose a topic from the list and write and illustrate a trickster tale that explains how the problem is solved. Decorate the front page of a newspaper to show the title "The Trickster Tribune," the date, and a class byline. Mount your students' completed projects on the newspaper pages. Laminate the pages for durability; then place the newspaper in your class library for all to read!

Coyote: A Trickster Tale From The American Southwest

Coyote finds mischief and mayhem wherever he goes. This time it's Coyote's boastful ways that land him in a heap of trouble.

Point out that stories such as Coyote's sometimes explain how something in nature came to be, or they teach a lesson or have a moral. Ask students why coyotes are no longer blue. Also find out if the youngsters think Coyote's tale taught a lesson or had a moral. For a fun writing assignment, ask each student to write and illustrate a legend that explains an occurrence in nature. Bind the students' stories into a class booklet.

Lisa Kelley—Gr. 1, James Walker Elementary, Blue Springs, MO

APPLAUSE FOR
ANGELA SHELF MEDEARIS

Usher your youngsters into the diverse world of Angela Shelf Medearis. From historical picture books to ghost stories to retellings of African folktales, this talented storyteller opens a window to the rich experiences and contributions of African-Americans. The following pages feature a sampling of the author's outstanding books along with several related classroom activities. Your students are sure to have plenty of applause for Ms. Medearis!

ideas contributed by Anne Bustard, Sharon Murphy, and Donna C. Kester Phillips

MEET THE AUTHOR

Angela Shelf Medearis, born November 16, 1956, has loved books and reading for as long as she can remember! Her father's career in the U.S. Air Force kept her family constantly on the move. But wherever their travels took them, Angela could always find her favorite books and a friendly face at the local library.

Medearis recalls her elementary school teachers praising her writing, but it wasn't until she was 30 years old and had begun to write professionally that the author realized her writing talent. Since then Medearis has published more than 20 children's books. Her writing is perhaps most widely recognized for its focus on African-American heritage. Her interest in history, her sensitivity to culture, and her love and concern for children give her writing a unique appeal that captivates and entertains young readers.

In addition to her writing, Medearis is the founder of and Project Director for Book Boosters. This multicultural, multiethnic program for all grade levels focuses on reading motivation, creative writing, and drama. Medearis also finds time to promote reading and writing by visiting schools and bookstores, and appearing at conferences throughout the country. When Medearis is not on the move, she can be found at home with her family in Austin, Texas.

THE ZEBRA-RIDING COWBOY

Illustrated by María Cristina Brusca
Henry Holt And Company, Inc.; 1992
In this brightly illustrated tale based on a western folk song, a bespectacled, educated fellow is mistaken for a greenhorn by a group of mischievous cowboys. The stranger not only proves his cowboy ability by riding the most ornery horse around, but he also reins in several stereotypes as well. Included in the back of the book is a note from the author that conjures up an image of what the real Old West was like.

After reading the book aloud, ask students to explain how the cowboys decided that the stranger was a green-horn. Encourage students to share times they have formed quick opinions about someone or something, only to discover that their opinions were incorrect. Then have each student write and illustrate a story in which he faces—and then overcomes—a situation in which he is misjudged. After students complete their stories, post them on a bulletin board covered with discarded newspapers. Then add the title "Special Edition: Overcoming Quick Judgments," the date, and a class byline to the board. A lot can be learned by reading these stories hot off the press!

Danny

We won!

Yesterday the teacher divided the class into two teams for our math fact game, but no one wanted me on his team. They said I would make a mistake and make the team lose a point. Instead I earned five points for them. Now everyone wants me on his team!

ANNIE'S GIFTS

Illustrated by Anna Rich
Just Us Books, Inc.; 1994

As a member of a musically talented family, Annie longs to play an instrument. But it doesn't matter which instrument Annie chooses, or how hard she tries to play it, the result is always the same—total disaster! Discouraged, yet determined, Annie never loses sight of finding her special talent. And in the end, she realizes that her special talent has been obvious to everyone but her!

Angela Shelf Medearis knows firsthand what it's like to grow up in a musically talented family and not be musically inclined. The inspiration for this heartwarming tale is a childhood memory! At the conclusion of the story, invite students to share their special talents. To do this, have each youngster trace a paper-doll template like the one shown onto construction paper, deco-rate the shape to resemble himself, and cut it out. Next have each student cut a heart shape from a two-inch square of construction paper, then personalize and label it with his special talent(s). To assemble his project, a student accordion-folds a 3/4" x 2 1/2" strip of paper; then he glues one end of the folded strip to the back of his heart cutout and the other end to the front of his self-likeness. Showcase the completed projects where others can take note of your multitalented youngsters!

Soccer Joe

THE SINGING MAN

Illustrated by Terea Shaffer
Holiday House, Inc.; 1995

In this adaptation of a West African folktale, a young man is banished from his village when he chooses to become a musician—an occupation that the elders say is unacceptable. With just a few coins in his pocket, a jug of water, a package of food, a flute, and a passion for music, the young man sets out to follow his dream. It is not until years later that others come to understand the wisdom of his choice.

As a prereading activity, play a variety of musical selections for your students' listening pleasure. Find out how each piece of music makes them feel. Then share the following quote from the story: "Yams fill the belly and trade fills the pockets, but music fills the heart." Ask students what the quote might mean. Then read the story aloud. At its conclusion invite students to summarize the story and further explain the meaning of the quote. Lead students to realize the importance of everyone's dreams for the future.

Next ask students what occupations their dreams for the future hold. List their responses on the chalkboard. Have each student choose a different career from the list, illustrate it on drawing paper, and write one sentence that explains the importance of the occupation at the bottom of his page. Bind the projects into a class booklet titled "Outstanding Occupa-tions," and place it in the classroom library for all to enjoy.

Jack

Construction workers build homes, stores, offices, and hospitals.

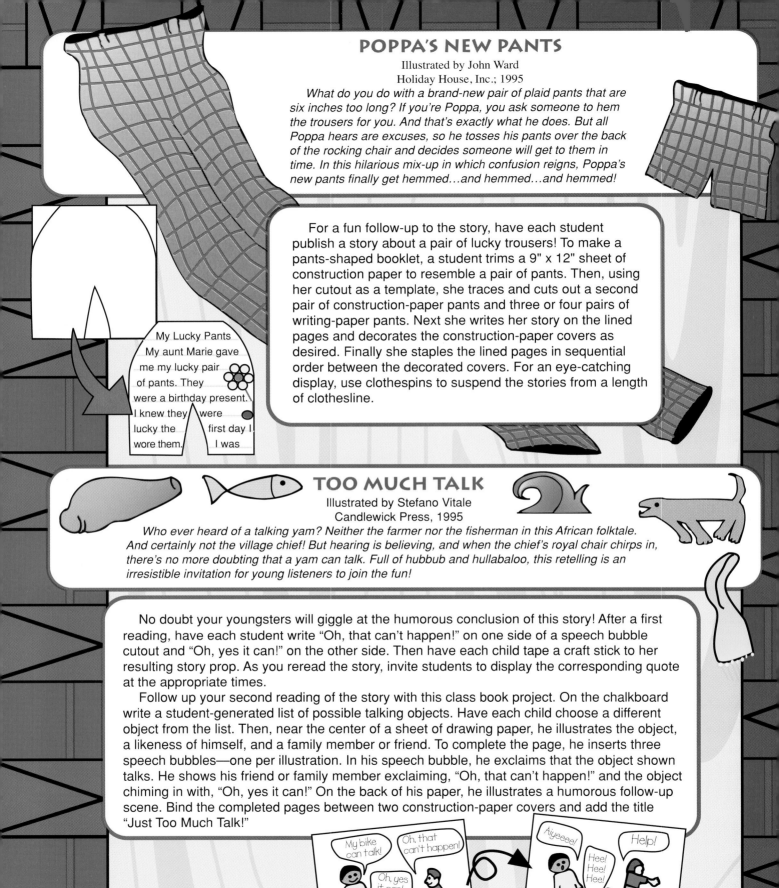

POPPA'S NEW PANTS

Illustrated by John Ward
Holiday House, Inc.; 1995

What do you do with a brand-new pair of plaid pants that are six inches too long? If you're Poppa, you ask someone to hem the trousers for you. And that's exactly what he does. But all Poppa hears are excuses, so he tosses his pants over the back of the rocking chair and decides someone will get to them in time. In this hilarious mix-up in which confusion reigns, Poppa's new pants finally get hemmed…and hemmed…and hemmed!

For a fun follow-up to the story, have each student publish a story about a pair of lucky trousers! To make a pants-shaped booklet, a student trims a 9" x 12" sheet of construction paper to resemble a pair of pants. Then, using her cutout as a template, she traces and cuts out a second pair of construction-paper pants and three or four pairs of writing-paper pants. Next she writes her story on the lined pages and decorates the construction-paper covers as desired. Finally she staples the lined pages in sequential order between the decorated covers. For an eye-catching display, use clothespins to suspend the stories from a length of clothesline.

My Lucky Pants
My aunt Marie gave me my lucky pair of pants. They were a birthday present. I knew they were lucky the first day I wore them. I was

TOO MUCH TALK

Illustrated by Stefano Vitale
Candlewick Press, 1995

Who ever heard of a talking yam? Neither the farmer nor the fisherman in this African folktale. And certainly not the village chief! But hearing is believing, and when the chief's royal chair chirps in, there's no more doubting that a yam can talk. Full of hubbub and hullabaloo, this retelling is an irresistible invitation for young listeners to join the fun!

No doubt your youngsters will giggle at the humorous conclusion of this story! After a first reading, have each student write "Oh, that can't happen!" on one side of a speech bubble cutout and "Oh, yes it can!" on the other side. Then have each child tape a craft stick to her resulting story prop. As you reread the story, invite students to display the corresponding quote at the appropriate times.

Follow up your second reading of the story with this class book project. On the chalkboard write a student-generated list of possible talking objects. Have each child choose a different object from the list. Then, near the center of a sheet of drawing paper, he illustrates the object, a likeness of himself, and a family member or friend. To complete the page, he inserts three speech bubbles—one per illustration. In his speech bubble, he exclaims that the object shown talks. He shows his friend or family member exclaiming, "Oh, that can't happen!" and the object chiming in with, "Oh, yes it can!" On the back of his paper, he illustrates a humorous follow-up scene. Bind the completed pages between two construction-paper covers and add the title "Just Too Much Talk!"

THE ADVENTURES OF SUGAR AND JUNIOR

Illustrated by Nancy Poydar
Holiday House, Inc.; 1995

In four easy-to-read chapter stories, the everyday adventures of two young friends are described. From shooting hoops to baking cookies to buying ice cream, the two friends enjoy each other's company. The friendship is an interracial one, but to these two friends, they couldn't be more alike. Students will relate to the activities and easily see themselves in roles these characters represent.

Try this fun follow-up activity for "The New Neighbors"—a story in which the two friends explain the origins of their names. Have each student write his first name and his nickname on individual index cards. (If a student does not have a nickname, he may choose one that he feels is appropriate.) Then, for a family-centered homework activity, ask students to interview their parents to find out more about their names. Instruct each student to record his parent's response for each name on the back of the corresponding card. When the cards are returned, collect the nickname cards and set them aside for later use. Then invite each student to share what he learned about his first name.

For a nickname-related activity, place the nickname cards in a container. One at a time, draw a card and read the name aloud. Then use the information on the back of the card to give students a clue or two about the classmate who bears this nickname. Each child who makes a guess must qualify his guess by explaining why he thinks the nickname being discussed fits the classmate he is suggesting. Return the cards to the students as their nicknames are revealed. Sharing your own nickname is sure to please the crowd!

Hector
I was named after my grandpa. He likes to garden. He has a big heart.

Tiger
My dad started calling me Tiger when I was a baby. He said I was loud! I think it is a good nickname for me now because I can run very fast!

THE GHOST OF SIFTY SIFTY SAM

Illustrated by Jacqueline Rogers
Scholastic Inc., 1997

To win a $5000 reward, a chef named Dan agrees to spend the night in a haunted house. Dan feels certain he's clever enough to outsmart the resident ghost, Sifty Sifty Sam. But when old Sifty shows himself, Dan can't keep himself from trembling with fear. In the end, it's not Dan that Sifty is interested in—it's Dan's cooking! Moonlit scenes and shadowy images dance across the pages of this rollicking rhyme.

Talking about real and imagined fears is a natural lead-in to this spooky story. Invite interested students to tell their classmates about one of their scariest moments. Then dim the lights and read the story aloud. As a follow-up to the story, pair students and challenge each twosome to write a recipe for a one-of-a-kind fish batter that Sifty Sifty Sam is sure to love. Have each pair write its recipe and fish-frying instructions on a large fish cut from bulletin-board paper. Display the projects around the room. There's something fishy going on around here!

First-Class Fish Batter
Ingredients:
flour   soda pop   catsup
salt   onions   lemon juice

Directions:
Mix the ingredients in a big bowl! Use the same amount of each. When the fizzing stops, dip the fish in the batter. Then fry the fish until it is very, very crunchy.

★ The Magic Of ★
ROBERT MUNSCH

Step into the wonderful world of Robert Munsch with this selection of stories and the activities that accompany them. You'll be glad you did!

The World According To Munsch

The key to Robert Munsch's success is his love for kids, something that is clearly obvious the minute he steps in front of a live audience. Robert is a master storyteller, but his entry into the field of storytelling was somewhat unconventional. He studied for seven years to become a Jesuit priest and anthropological missionary. Along the way he picked up degrees in American history, anthropology, and early childhood education. But it was in a part-time job at a day-care center that he discovered he loved working with youngsters. Here he began telling stories as a way to quiet the children at naptime, and he quickly learned what worked and what didn't.

Before Munsch publishes a story, he tells it over and over again to different groups of youngsters. His rule of thumb is that if a story is good now, it will be even better in a few more years. So, with the help of his young fans, he hones his stories until they are "just right." Then they are ready to be published.

Robert Munsch lives with his wife and three adopted children in Guelph, Ontario, Canada.

Thomas' Snowsuit

Illustrated by Michael Martchenko
Published by Annick Press Ltd.

Where else but in a Munsch story can you find a male principal and a female teacher unwittingly switching clothes? So is the case in this outrageous tale about a boy who absolutely hates the new snowsuit his mother has purchased for him—or so it seems.

For a lively follow-up discussion, ask youngsters to tell about clothing they dislike. If desired, list the youngsters' names and clothing choices on the chalkboard. Then retell the story, replacing Thomas and his snowsuit with the name and clothing choice of a student. The hilarious results will be applauded by your youngsters. Next divide students into small groups and have each group member retell the tale featuring himself as the main story character.

From **THOMAS' SNOWSUIT by Robert Munsch**. Art copyright © Michael Martchenko, 1985. Reprinted by arrangement with Annick Press Ltd.

Moira's Birthday

Illustrated by Michael Martchenko
Published by Annick Press Ltd.

In this zany story a child's fantasy and a parent's nightmare come true. Moira has permission to invite six youngsters to her birthday party. But, not wanting to hurt anyone's feelings, Moira invites another child and another child and another child. Soon, unbeknownst to her parents, Moira's small birthday celebration has become a schoolwide affair.

At the conclusion of the story, have students recall the challenges that Moira encountered and solved during and after her party. Ask youngsters if they think the party turned out as Moira had hoped it would. Then have youngsters predict what Moira might plan for her next birthday celebration. At the end of the discussion, serve cupcakes and punch in honor of Moira's birthday. Invite students to share their ideas for creating the best birthday party ever.

Mortimer

Illustrated by Michael Martchenko
Published by Annick Press Ltd.

When it's bedtime for Mortimer, everyone in the household knows. You see, Mortimer has this bedtime song that he sings and sings and sings. Mother can't stop his singing. Father can't stop his singing. Mortimer's 17 brothers and sisters can't stop his singing. Even two tough-looking policemen can't stop Mortimer's singing. Will Mortimer ever go to sleep?

This rollicking tale is the very first story that Robert Munsch ever created. And just like so many other Munsch tales, this one is highly contagious. In no time at all, students will be chiming in on familiar verses and phrases. At the conclusion of the story, list the people who visited Mortimer that evening. Next have students brainstorm other parties that could have paid him a visit. Your list might include three official firemen, the city mayor, and the local veterinarian. Continue the list until you have one visiting party per student. Then have each youngster illustrate a different scene from the list. Compile the illustrations into a booklet entitled "Mortimer Sings On!" Then, with your youngsters' help, tell this sequel to *Mortimer*.

Show And Tell

Illustrated by Michael Martchenko
Published by Annick Press Ltd.

Searching for the perfect show-and-tell item can be quite challenging, but this time Ben has found a winner—his new baby sister. Excited about his discovery, he quickly tucks his tiny sister inside his knapsack and scurries off to school. Before long his baby sister begins to cry and cry and cry. Doesn't anyone at school know what to do with a crying baby? Apparently not!

A master at telling stories, Munsch believes his success is greatly due to the fact that he tells and writes stories about the real concerns of young children. For example youngsters worry about basic things such as avoiding bedtime *(Mortimer),* going to the bathroom *(I Have To Go!),* and selecting perfect show-and-tell items. He is also quick to point out that his books are successful because of their quality illustrations. As a follow-up to this hilarious story, have each youngster illustrate what he would consider to be the perfect item for show-and-tell. Be sure to review the final illustration of the book with your students before they begin. Artist Michael Martchenko has a few ideas of his own that your youngsters just might recognize!

Pigs

Illustrated by Michael Martchenko
Published by Annick Press Ltd.

In part, youngsters love Munsch stories because his kid characters routinely get away with the kinds of stuff they long to get away with. In this delightfully silly tale, Megan has been clearly warned to not open the gate to the pig pen. But Megan takes matters into her own hands and decides that the pigs are so dumb they'd just stand there even if she did open the gate—just a teeny tiny bit. Oink! Oink!

Even though Megan's father warned her to not be fooled by the pigs, Megan's curiosity got the best of her. Take a student poll to find out how many students think Megan would have left the gate alone if her father had not mentioned it. Invite students to share their reasoning. Then have students make and pig out on these scrumptious ice-cream treats. To make a little piggy like the one shown, place a rounded scoop of strawberry ice cream in a foil muffin cup. For each ear, insert one corner of a small square cracker into the ice cream. Add a miniature-marshmallow snout, two chocolate-chip eyes, and a piece of red licorice for a tail. As students devour their desserts, have them ponder what kind of mischief Megan may get into next.

Lona Ritchie—Gr. 3 and Lesley Kurre—Gr. 1, Perry County District #32, Cape Girardeau, MO

The Paper Bag Princess

Illustrated by Michael Martchenko
Published by Annick Press Ltd.

Here is a turnabout fable that is loved by both children and adults. Youngsters love the fact that a small princess outsmarts a big fiery dragon. And adults applaud the story because it is a nonsexist fairy tale in which the prince is saved by the princess—who in the end decides that the prince is just a shallow bum in fancy clothes and not worth marrying after all!

Being a master storyteller, Munsch never sees his stories as finished once and for all. It's not unusual for him to telephone his publishers after the book has gone to press to tell them he's rewritten the ending—again. Such is the case with *The Paper Bag Princess*. Over the years, Munsch has continued to perfect the story for his audiences, making changes to the original printed version. Find out what changes, additions, and deletions your youngsters would make to and from the story if they were given the opportunity to rewrite it. Then have each student write a personalized version of *The Paper Bag Princess*. When the stories and illustrations are completed, have each student design a cover for his story using a paper bag and markers. Younger students will enjoy doing this activity as a class project.

A Promise Is A Promise

Written by Robert Munsch & Michael Kusugak
Illustrated by Vladyana Krykorka
Published by Annick Press Ltd.

Loosely based on Inuit legend and a childhood experience of coauthor Michael Kusugak, the suspense in this story makes it unique from other Munsch tales. Ignoring her mother's advice, a young Inuit girl ventures onto the sea ice where she is captured by Qallupilluit—ghostly monsters that live beneath the frozen surface. She finally escapes the monsters but only after she promises to bring them all of her brothers and sisters. A promise is a promise....

Explain to students that the Inuit invented the imaginary Qallupilluit in an attempt to keep their children from wandering onto the dangerous sea ice. For a monstrously fun follow-up, have students brainstorm health and safety reminders that they often hear from adults. Write the reminders on the chalkboard and discuss the importance of each one. After each child has chosen a reminder that he frequently forgets, have him design a poster such as the one shown to make him be more mindful of the adult advice.

Did you brush your teeth?

I ♥ DIRTY TEETH!

Love You Forever

Illustrated by Sheila McGraw
Published by Firefly Books Ltd.

Adults and children respond differently to this heartfelt story. The story tells of a mother's steadfast love for her son through all the stages of his growth. Each night she coos him to sleep with a special lullaby. With the passage of time, their roles reverse and it is the son who sings to his ailing mother. From most adults the story evokes feelings of sadness and loss. Youngsters, on the other hand, often find humor in the role reversal that takes place. Munsch admits that even though it is his best-selling book, it is not typically requested by children.

At the conclusion of the story, ask your students to list the people who they feel love them unconditionally. Then have each child write and deliver a letter of thanks to one person on her list. Invite students to repeat the activity daily until each person on their lists has been thanked.

Purple, Green And Yellow

Illustrated by Hélène Desputeaux
Published by Annick Press Ltd.

While at the 1990 Toronto Storytelling Festival, Munsch noticed a young girl named Brigid who was painting her fingernails with colored markers. Inspired by Brigid and her coloring habits, Munsch spun a colorful tale about a young girl and her markers. After approximately two years of honing the story with the help of his young fans, *Purple, Green And Yellow* was ready to be published. This wacky tale will undoubtedly be a hit with your youngsters.

Create an eye-catching display entitled "This One's For Brigid!" at the conclusion of this colorful story. Cut a length of white bulletin-board paper to fit your display area. Cut the paper into puzzle pieces, one per student. (If desired, number the pieces for easy reassembling.) Then, using watercolor markers, have each student color his puzzle piece as desired. Reassemble the puzzle and staple the pieces to the display. Cut the title from black construction paper and mount it atop the eye-catching artwork. Wow! Your students are artists!

More Munsch Books

Robert Munsch has published over 20 children's books. Ask your librarian for assistance in locating additional stories by this famous author.

From **MOIRA'S BIRTHDAY by Robert Munsch.**
Art copyright © Michael Martchenko, 1987.
Reprinted by arrangement with Annick Press Ltd.

IF YOU GIVE
LAURA JOFFE NUMEROFF
A PENCIL,...

...You can expect a delightful story! Use these ideas to extend your students' enjoyment of Laura Joffe Numeroff's deliciously kid-pleasing tales.

IF YOU GIVE A MOUSE A COOKIE

Illustrated by Felicia Bond
Scholastic Inc., 1985

Would you give a cookie to a mouse? Without realizing what this gesture could lead to, a little boy does just that. The mouse then requests a glass of milk and follows the boy into his home. Once inside the house, the mouse's requests escalate, with each request becoming a bit zanier than the one that preceded it. Before long the mouse has worked up quite a thirst, so it's back to more milk—and, that's right—another cookie!

Numeroff came up with the story of *If You Give A Mouse A Cookie* to amuse herself during a long, boring car ride. Interestingly enough, her story—which has since won numerous awards—was rejected by several publishing houses before it was finally accepted for publication. Inspire your youngsters to write their own award-winning mouse tales with these easy-to-make mouse booklets. To make a booklet, fold an 18" x 6" piece of gray construction paper in half. To form the nose, cut to round the bottom corners of the front cover. Cut out and glue two mouse ears along the fold; then add construction-paper whiskers and facial features. To complete the booklet, staple several 5 1/2" x 8" sheets of paper between the booklet covers. So what might Numeroff's cookie-eating and milk-drinking mouse be up to next?

What do you think will happen if you give a mouse some math? Students will find out at this math-related center. Number and program several construction-paper cookie cutouts with desired math problems. For each cookie, program a small dessert plate with its corresponding answer; then program the bottoms of the plates for self-checking. Place the cookies, the plates, and a mouse cutout at a center. Provide scratch paper and pencils if appropriate. A student places each cookie on its corresponding plate; then he peeks under the plates to check his work.

Erin Hoffman—Gr. 1, Cumru Elementary School, Shillington, PA

seven tens
six ones

two tens
one one

three tens
four ones

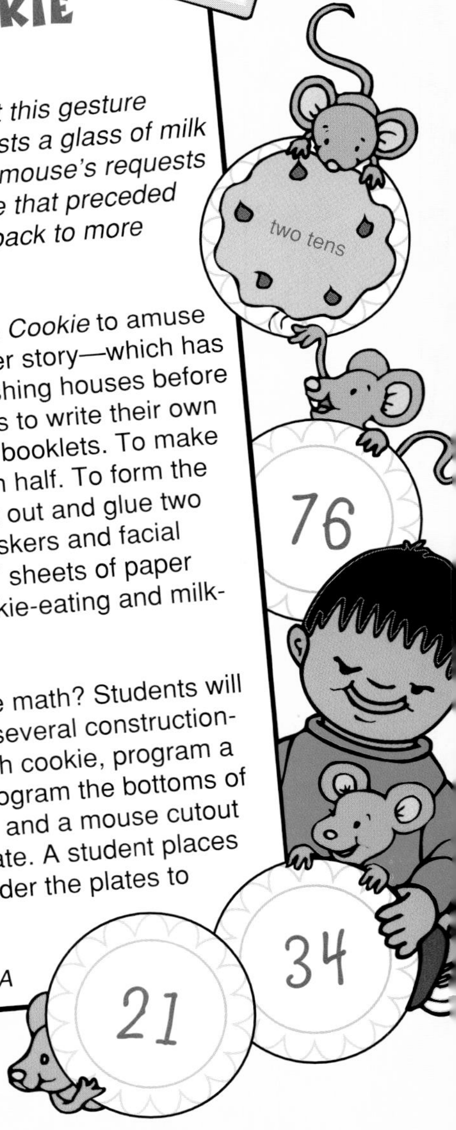

two tens

76

21

34

IF YOU GIVE A MOOSE A MUFFIN

Illustrated by Felicia Bond
Scholastic Inc., 1991

If you set muffins on a windowsill, you'd better be prepared to give one to a friendly moose that has caught the scent. In this rollicking tale, a boy does give a moose a muffin—setting the wheels in motion for a series of hilarious events that get wackier at each turn of the page. Never has the phrase "Please don't feed the animals" been more appropriate!

Collect a few props—such as a muffin tin, an empty muffin mix box, an empty jam container, a sweater, a few pieces of cardboard, and a bedsheet—and you'll have just what you need to dramatize this delightful story. Select one student volunteer to be the moose and one to be the boy. Follow up the theatrics by asking students to imagine how the story might have been different if—instead of a moose coming to the windowsill—it were a magpie (macaw, mole, mouse, musk ox, mongoose) that came to visit. Perhaps some more theatrics are in order?

Your youngsters will be eager to make these moose puppets. Ask each youngster to bring a discarded sock (preferably brown in color) from home. To make a puppet, cut two antlers, two eyes, and a bell from construction paper. Then use fabric glue to attach these cutouts to the sock as shown above. No doubt these moose puppets will be on the lookout for some sweet-smelling muffins!

MOUSE COOKIES: 10 EASY-TO-MAKE COOKIE RECIPES WITH A STORY IN PICTURES

Illustrated by Felicia Bond
HarperFestival®, 1995

The mouse from *If You Give A Mouse A Cookie* is back, and this time he's brought his ten favorite cookie recipes with him! This spiral-bound collection of easy-to-bake recipes includes a mouse-shaped cookie cutter and a brand-new story that's told using only pictures. The boy, who has found the mouse's house in the base of a tree trunk, peeks through a small window and discovers that the mouse is up to his elbows in cookie dough. Unfortunately the first batch of cookies burns—but from that point on, cookies, cookies, and more cookies are pulled from the oven and eaten by the mouse. However, before the mouse eats all the cookies himself, he hands one out the window to the boy.

It's a must! There's no way around it! If a mouse can bake cookies, so can your youngsters. With the help of a parent volunteer, plan for your students to bake and sample two or more different cookie recipes from this book. Then create a class graph to show which mouse cookie is voted the top choice by your youngsters.

DOGS DON'T WEAR SNEAKERS

Illustrated by Joe Mathieu
Simon & Schuster Books For Young Readers, 1993

"Dogs don't wear sneakers/And pigs don't wear hats/And dresses look silly/On Siamese cats." So goes Laura Joffe Numeroff's lively, laugh-along text that explores the many ways in which humans differ from their furry, feathered, and finned friends. Hilarious illustrations bring Numeroff's unlikely creatures roaring to life.

On the final page of the book, the author invites her readers to extend this deliriously funny dream themselves. So why not do just that? On the chalkboard write two student-generated lists of animals—animals that appear in the book and animals that do not. Also brainstorm a third class list of things animals can't do. Then, on provided drawing paper, have each child illustrate an animal doing something that it could only do in a dream and add appropriate text. Bind the resulting booklet pages between construction-paper covers. If desired feature the poem at the right on the front cover.

And pigs don't dance cheek to cheek!

We closed our eyes
And we drew with our minds.
And we were surprised
By what we did find!

And hedgehogs will never be king!

CHIMPS DON'T WEAR GLASSES

Illustrated by Joe Mathieu
Simon & Schuster Books For Young Readers, 1995

Numeroff and Mathieu have combined their talents again to create an adorably funny sequel to Dogs Don't Wear Sneakers. Hang-gliding horses, ice-skating tigers, and zebras that cook are just a few of the playful happenings in this imaginative menagerie of animals.

Once again Numeroff invites her readers to continue the outrageous ordeals that she has begun. For a unique twist on this invitation, why not rewrite the author's book by replacing each featured animal with a different animal name that has the same number of syllables. (For example, "Chimps don't wear glasses/And zebras don't cook/And you won't see a kangaroo reading a book" could be rewritten as "Skunks don't wear glasses/And penguins don't cook/And you won't see an *elephant* reading a book.") Once the text has been created, copy it onto large sheets of paper and have the students illustrate the resulting booklet pages. Bind the pages between poster-board covers. This big book is sure to be a big hit with your students!

WHY A DISGUISE?

Illustrated by David McPhail
Simon & Schuster Books For Young Readers, 1996
In Numeroff's latest romp, a young boy discovers the dos and don'ts of donning a disguise. This funny slice-of-life tale will have your students laughing all the way to the costume shop!

For a fun-filled follow-up to this delightful story, have each youngster create a homemade disguise. Enlist your students' help in writing a parent letter that includes a brief summary of the book and a request for disguise-making materials. Ask that all donations be brought to school by a specified date. Then have each child copy the letter and carry it home. In the meantime gather an assortment of worn-out shirts, hats, scarves, and other appropriate disguise-making articles to add to those that your students will bring to school. You will also need a supply of plastic grocery bags. On the day of the disguise-making event, plan to have your students visit neighboring classrooms incognito. Then photograph each disguised child. Students can carry home their disguises in plastic grocery bags and, when appropriate, don the disguises for their families.

This bulletin board is sure to receive rave reviews! Title the display "Why A Disguise?" On the top half of a sheet of paper, have each child illustrate himself incognito. Then have each child answer the question "Why a disguise?" on the bottom half of his paper. Or mount each child's photograph from the previous activity on the bulletin board and have the students write their answers on writing paper. Mount the students' papers alongside their photographs. Either way this display is sure to attract quite a lot of attention!

Georgia

Why A Disguise?
So my little brother Kenny won't try to sit next to me in the cafeteria!

ABOUT THE AUTHOR

Laura Joffe Numeroff grew up in a world of books, music, and art. As a result she began drawing and writing at an early age. As she says, "I've been drawing pictures since I was old enough to hold a crayon, and writing came soon after. Doing children's books combines the two things I love the most." Books have always been an integral part of Numeroff's life. As a child, she would bring home books from her local library—often immersing herself in one author's work. Among Numeroff's favorite authors were Beverly Cleary, Marguerite Henry, and A. A. Milne. Even today she proclaims herself to be a "read-a-holic," with a penchant for biographies, especially those about other writers.

Numeroff began her successful writing career attending Pratt Institute in Brooklyn, New York. She has written and illustrated over a dozen children's books to date. She is probably most well known for her best-selling *If You Give A Mouse A Cookie* and *If You Give A Moose A Muffin.* In addition to her writing, Numeroff has had some interesting jobs that include being a private investigator and operating a merry-go-round! As a child she even walked dogs for money. In her spare time, Numeroff can often be found in libraries or bookstores. She is an avid collector of children's books—especially autographed copies. Numeroff also enjoys collecting rubber stamps and snow shakers, listening to music, dancing, and eating Cajun food. And she sees a lot of movies too. In one year alone, she saw 72!

Born on July 14, 1953, in Brooklyn, New York, this delightful author now resides in Los Angeles, California.

Bill Peet Is Hard To Beat!

Bill Peet's wonderful children's books have been cheered by young and old alike. In this collection you'll find activities to accompany just a small sampling of the more than 30 books that Peet has created for his many fans all over the world. Enjoy!

ideas by Kimberly A. Spring

About The Author

What a success story Bill Peet's life has been! In *Bill Peet: An Autobiography* (Houghton Mifflin Company), Peet uses words and pictures to tell the fascinating tale of his life. Any fans of Bill Peet will find this treasury of information irresistible.

Hubert's Hair-Raising Adventure

Published by Houghton Mifflin Company
Haughty and proud, Hubert the lion suffers a dreadful blow to his ego when his mane catches on fire and his hair is reduced to stubble. Thanks to his animal friends and a few crocodile tears, Hubert returns to glory with a perfectly square mane.

Before students hear the complete story about Hubert, engage them in some problem solving. Read the first eight pages, ending with Elephant's observation:

"It will never grow back, you can be pretty sure,
Unless we can manage to think of some cure."

At this point, pair students and challenge each twosome to invent a cure for Hubert's baldness. When the students have identified the necessary ingredients and/or procedures they will use, have each pair either design a poster or present a commercial advertising its cure. Without a doubt, these projects and performances will be most memorable!

Although Hubert fails to learn from his lesson in humility, students will adore his pursuit and the faithful friends who support him. Make a student-generated character web for Hubert and another for the kind-hearted Elephant. Ask students to describe the similarities and the differences between these two characters. In conclusion, find out how many students would prefer Hubert as a friend. Elephant as a friend? Why?

The Whingdingdilly

Published by Houghton Mifflin Company
Feeling unloved and insignificant, Scamp, a once-carefree hound, trades his dog's life for that of a whingdingdilly. His search for fame and admiration comes to a screeching halt when he discovers that he has become nothing more than a feared and ridiculed spectacle.

Plan to read Scamp's adventure in two sittings. Conclude the first reading on page 21, taking care to conceal all illustrations featuring Scamp's transformation into a whingdingdilly. As a follow-up activity, have students recall the magic Zildy performed on Scamp. List these changes on the board; then have students refer to the list as they complete their own whingdingdilly renderings. Students will enjoy comparing their illustrations to those of a professional...Bill Peet!

At the conclusion of the story, ask students what they think Scamp learned from his dilly of an adventure. Point out that Scamp had forgotten all about his fine sense of direction, and ask students to brainstorm traits and talents that they may have overlooked in themselves. For a fun letter-writing activity, have each student compose a letter to Scamp. Suggest that students welcome Scamp home in their letters, and tell him about the special qualities they have rediscovered in themselves.

The Wump World

Published by Houghton Mifflin Company

The Wumps are living a simple, idyllic life in Wump World until the day the Pollutians invade their planet. Before long the Wump World's serene environment is replaced with huge cities, busy freeways, and intolerable pollution. Recognizing only that their world has gone sour, the Pollutians blast off to repeat their mistakes elsewhere, leaving behind a small shadow of hope for the once-content Wumps.

Bill Peet's deceptively straightforward environmental message will not go unnoticed by your students. Under your youngsters' direction, list ways the Pollutians damaged the Wumps' environment. Entitle the collection "Problems" and as a group discuss possible solutions for each one. Then, working in pairs, have students write newspaper articles for a special edition of the *Wump World Report*. In each article students should describe a problem created by the Pollutians and propose a solution that could help restore and protect the environment of Wump World. Mount the completed projects on lengths of bulletin-board paper that have been folded and labeled to resemble a newspaper.

Mounds Of Garbage Left Behind!

The Pollutians invaded Wump World and left piles of garbage everywhere. There is even garbage in the water!

At a town meeting, the Wumps voted to clean up the environment. From this moment on, all Wump trash will be recycled. Wump volunteers will work to gather and recycle the trash that the Pollutians left behind.

Eli

Published by Houghton Mifflin Company

Eli, a decrepit old lion, has become too timid to fend for himself among the other lions. So he manages to get by on the other lions' leftovers which he reluctantly shares with a squawking, squabbling flock of vultures. He thinks they are despicable creatures that he will never learn to like. But quite by accident, he saves Vera Vulture's neck, and to show her gratitude she and the rest of her flock return the favor.

Eli eventually became grateful for his friends the vultures. Discuss with your students the types of things that make friendships grow. Then have each child create a friendship recipe like the one shown. Provide time for students to share their recipes for lasting friendships.

Recipe For Friendship
Ingredients:
1 cup caring
1 cup dependability
pinch of risk
1 cup understanding
1 cup honesty

Mix all ingredients together for ever and ever!

Bill Peet describes Eli as "meek as a mouse." Be sure your youngsters understand the meaning of this phrase before challenging them to brainstorm other animal-related similes like "as slow as a turtle," "as silly as a monkey," and "as clever as a porpoise." Post the resulting list of similes at a writing center. Encourage students to use these and other similes in their writing for added interest and detail. Or have each student copy and illustrate a different simile from the list; then compile the pages into a class simile booklet.

Chester The Worldly Pig

Published by Houghton Mifflin Company

Chester is one little pig who isn't going to market—at least if he can help it! After hours of practice, Chester perfects his own special trick and joins the circus. But his aspiration of becoming a star performer vanishes when he encounters unbearable humiliation. Next a series of near-fatal mishaps force Chester to return to the trough and succumb to a pig's life. For a normal pig, that might have resulted in a visit to the meat market. But not for Chester—the one and only worldly pig!

For a unique geography lesson, have students create these worldly pig projects! To begin, each student needs two large, identical ovals cut from pink paper and a white construction-paper copy of the seven continents on page 92. Have each youngster color and cut out the continents. Providing assistance as needed, have students mount their cutouts atop the ovals, creating two halves of a simplistic world map. After students have labeled desired geographic locations, demonstrate how to join the two ovals to create a "world map." If a three-dimensional effect is desired, staple the outer edge of the project, leaving an opening along the lower rim; then stuff the project with crumpled newspaper and staple the opening closed. To complete the project, each student designs and attaches a head, feet, and a tail to his worldly pig. If desired, suspend the projects from the ceiling.

Your students shouldn't be at a loss for words when asked to generate descriptions of Chester and his actions. Bored, clever, persistent, disappointed, silly, and embarrassed are only a few of the many possibilities. List the words provided by your youngsters on the chalkboard. Then, in turn, have students secretly choose and pantomime a word or a phrase from the list for her classmates to identify. Vocabularies and dramatic skills are sure to blossom!

There's No Such Thing!

No Such Things

Published by Houghton Mifflin Company

In the rhythmic verse his fans adore, Bill Peet has created a book filled with a menagerie of fanciful beasts that will tickle your youngsters' funny bones. From the Mopwoggins, who hide their bald heads with their fuzzy tails, to the snickering Snoof who leaves backward tracks in the snow, students will enthusiastically resound, "There's no such thing!"

After reading this one-of-a-kind fantasy, create an eye-catching display entitled "There's No Such Thing!" To do this, have each student illustrate an animal of his own imagination and pen a descriptive paragraph about the creature. Suggest that students describe where the animals live, what they eat, their habits, and their special talents. Mount the completed projects on the display.

The Spooky Tail Of Prewitt Peacock

Published by Houghton Mifflin Company

With only a few scrawny feathers, Prewitt is the least regarded peacock in his flock. And when his plumage grows into what looks like a wild-eyed monster, he is even further alienated from the other birds. But when the peacocks encounter their arch rival, Travis, it is Prewitt's scary tail that sends the tiger running.

Undoubtedly your students will have lots of advice for Phineas and the other proud peacocks. Allow time for students to discuss how the flock behaved toward poor Prewitt. Do they think that he deserved to be outcast? Why or why not? Also find out what advice your youngsters would give Prewitt. Finally invite youngsters to describe times when they have felt unjustly treated. As a class discuss these situations and brainstorm how similar situations could be handled or avoided.

Farewell To Shady Glade

Published by Houghton Mifflin Company

When the rumbling noises first began, the woodland creatures of Shady Glade were concerned, but not alarmed. They felt that nothing could ever spoil their perfect home along the wooded creek bank. But when the raccoon scampers to the top of the towering sycamore searching for reassurance, he discovers that he and his friends are doomed. Monstrous machines, leaving nothing but barren earth in their tracks, are headed straight for Shady Glade! With no time to lose, the raccoon contrives a plan to move the small band of inhabitants to a safe place.

In preparation for this follow-up activity, have youngsters discuss the kinds of things the animals in the story needed in their environment to survive. If desired, write their suggestions on the chalkboard. Next divide students into small groups and give each group a section of white bulletin-board paper. Challenge each group to illustrate a desirable environment for a group of animals. Explain that the animals must be included in the illustration and that each environment must have a name. For added appeal, have students complete the artwork using colored pencils, just as Bill Peet did! When the projects are finished, display them for all to see. Several days later, have each student write an environmental tale to accompany one of the illustrations.

Big Bad Bruce

Published by Houghton Mifflin Company

Big Bad Bruce, the bear bully, is justly brought down to size, but not before he terrifies the whole forest. Fed up with his mischief, Roxy, the witch, cooks up a blueberry pie filled with a magic shrinking potion and feeds it to the bear. When Bruce awakens from his snooze, he is no longer big and bad. Instead he is small and frightened!

When the story ends, tiny Bruce is once again up to his old bullying ways. Now he's intimidating the grasshoppers, beetles, and caterpillars. Challenge students to think of ways for the bugs to solve their problems with Bruce. Have each student write and illustrate his solution. Invite students to share their creative remedies with their classmates.

Patterns

Use with *Chester The Worldly Pig* on page 90.

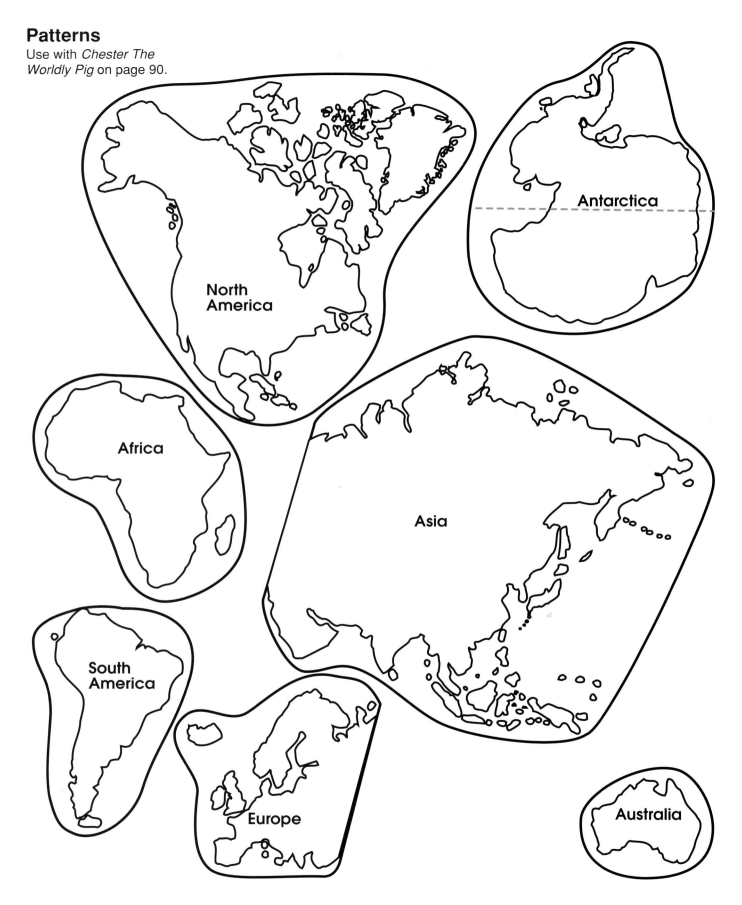

North America

Antarctica

Africa

Asia

South America

Europe

Australia

Note To The Teacher: To correctly position the continent of Antarctica on the pig project, have each student cut apart his Antarctica cutout (on the dotted line) before gluing the continent in place. (See the illustration on page 90.)

"Why Should I Waste A Perfectly Good Story On You?"

Patricia Polacco And Her Books

Forty-some years ago, Patricia Polacco's grandmother strolled around an enormous rock in her front yard. "Do you want to know how this got here?" she asked. Patricia looked at the rock and said, "Well, Bubee, that's a rock." "Well, if a rock is all you can see, what a pity! It means you have no imagination. If you have no imagination, why should I waste a perfectly good story on you?" So Patricia said, "Hasn't it always been there?" During the conversation that ensued, Patricia Polacco's grandmother told her the story of a falling star which was the inspiration for *Meteor!*, her first book.

Even though Patricia's grandmother died before her fifth birthday, her storytelling (and that of other family members, including her dad) had a profound effect on Patricia. Much of Patricia Polacco's writing is based on experiences she had on her grandmother's farm in Union City, Michigan. After her grandmother's death, Patricia's family moved to Oakland, California, to a neighborhood characterized by a mix of cultures, races, and religions. It was there that she met her lifelong friend, Stewart Washington. *Chicken Sunday* is Patricia's book about Stewart's family.

In Patricia's family, when a child was about to read, it was customary to put a drop of honey on the cover of the book. The message that this symbolized was that, like honey, knowledge is sweet. Like the bee from which the honey came, knowledge may be elusive. But if you chase it through the pages of books, it will finally be yours. For Patricia, the chase was an especially difficult one, since she had undiagnosed learning disabilities. When she was 14, a teacher discovered this well-guarded secret and paid for Patricia to have twice-weekly sessions with a reading specialist. Years later, Patricia's high school English teacher ridiculed her spelling, but admitted, "...you *do* tell a good story!" The overwhelming majority of people who have read her books can't testify to her poor spelling, but most wholeheartedly agree that she definitely tells a good story.

Use the ideas on the next four pages to introduce your youngsters to Patricia Polacco's stories.

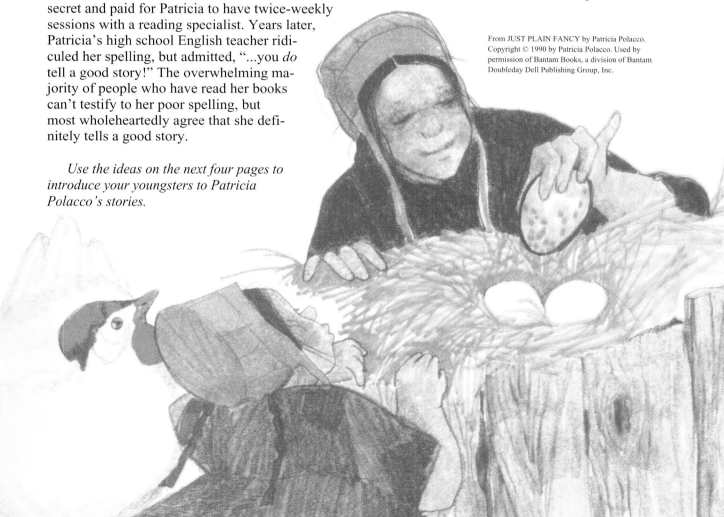

From JUST PLAIN FANCY by Patricia Polacco. Copyright © 1990 by Patricia Polacco. Used by permission of Bantam Books, a division of Bantam Doubleday Dell Publishing Group, Inc.

Meteor!

Published by G. P. Putnam

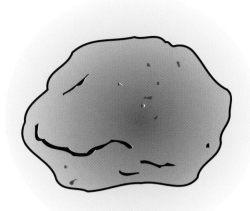

It seems fitting that Patricia Polacco's version of her grandmother's falling-star story became her first children's book. Patricia, at the age of 41, seemed to fall from nowhere right smack-dab into the mainstream of children's literature. Like the rock around which *Meteor!* pivots, Patricia Polacco is a source of wonder. Reading *Meteor!* is a great way to introduce your youngsters to this author and her work.

You may want to draw students into the story much like Grandma Gaw drew Patricia into it (see page 93). Gather students around a rock, and ask what they see. Ask them to imagine that this rock has an unusual past and presently seems to have magical powers. Explain that perhaps this rock is part of the original stone which once held the magical sword in the medieval story *Sword In The Stone.* After discussing this possibility, ask volunteers to speculate about other extraordinary circumstances which could have involved the rock, making it extraordinarily special. Then explain that this rock is not unlike the one in Patricia Polacco's story. After reading *Meteor!* aloud, mention that sometimes when the author talks to groups of students, she brings along a piece of the real meteor on which this story is based. It's her way of encouraging youngsters to see the extraordinary in the ordinary.

The Keeping Quilt

Published by Simon And Schuster Books For Young Readers

Patricia Polacco's Great-Gramma Anna came to America with her Russian family. To preserve the memories of the people they had left behind, Anna's mother made a quilt using fabric from Anna's babushka and also pieces of clothing which belonged to their relatives in "backhome" Russia. Over the years, the quilt became an important part of family celebrations. Find out if any of your youngsters have a similar family keepsake. Send copies of a note to parents (and other relatives) encouraging them to talk to youngsters about the origins of these items, so that youngsters may share this information with their classmates. As students share what they've learned from their family discussions, acknowledge the diverse family backgrounds that your youngsters bring to your class.

Tricia Reiser—Gr. 3
Ware Elementary
Ft. Riley, KS

When Patricia Polacco speaks to teachers, she sometimes tells the story of *The Keeping Quilt* and displays the real keeping quilt, parts of which are 120 years old. Each of the colorful pieces of fabric represents a series of memories and generations of forebears that have been symbolically pieced together to represent who she is and what she holds dear. When talking about children, she draws the analogy that each teacher's influence is indelibly sewn into the souls of their students forever—much like the pieces in the keeping quilt.

Help your youngsters preserve the memories of this school year with a photo quilt. Have students arrange photos taken throughout the year on a piece of bulletin-board paper. After youngsters use rubber cement to glue the photos in place, have them draw stitches around the photos to resemble quilting. Permanent markers, paint pens, or colored glues may be used to draw the stitching. Display this class keeping quilt and encourage students to recall the memories of the year.

Karen Berryhill—Gr. 3
Aikin Elementary
Paris, TX

After reading *The Keeping Quilt,* ask each youngster to bring a favorite quilt or blanket to school with his parent's permission. Encourage youngsters to wrap up in their blankets or quilts and talk about different uses for them and the variety of textures, colors, and designs they represent. As a story memento, present each student with a small square of material symbolic of a quilt piece. Encourage youngsters to write about a favored blanket or quilt. (Stories may be fiction, if desired.) Then allow time for students to share the warm memories they've recorded.

Karen Berryhill—Gr. 3

Thunder Cake

Published by Philomel Books

Here's a marvelous way to set the mood for *Thunder Cake.* Spread one acrylic blanket on the floor; then spread another on top of the first one. Lift the top blanket several times until static electricity is generated. Play a recording of thunder, if one is available. Darken your classroom. Lift the top blanket again, so that students can see the light show created by the blankets. Discuss thunder and lightning with your students.

To read the story, wear a scarf and shawl and sit in a rocking chair. (Rocking chairs are Patricia Polacco's favorite thinking places. There's one in almost every room of her house.) Play the thunder sounds softly as you read *Thunder Cake* aloud. Afterward permit youngsters to sample strawberries and pureed tomatoes, which are ingredients in Grandma's recipe. Then have youngsters assist you in preparing a Thunder Cake according to the directions at the back of the book.

Martha Nelson
Prosser School District
Prosser, WA

Thunder Cake is Patricia Polacco's story about the way her grandmother taught her to face and overcome her fear of thunder. This makes it an excellent read-aloud choice to open discussions about fears. After reading the book aloud, have children discuss things of which they are afraid. Then have students signify on a blank graph, the things that they fear. Discuss the resulting graph. Ask students to think of the grandmother in *Thunder Cake* and imagine what her response would be to the most prominent fear (or fears) on the graph. If desired, have volunteers take turns playing the role of the grandmother and explaining to the class the resources they have within themselves to overcome this fear.

adapted from an idea by Janet Lyon-Cardwell—Gr. 2
North Wilkesboro Elementary
North Wilkesboro, NC

Follow up a reading of *Thunder Cake* and a discussion of fears with this creative-thinking activity. Remind students that making a Thunder Cake helped Patricia overcome her fear of thunder. Then ask each student to name a dessert that could be used to help someone overcome a specific fear. (If you made the graph mentioned in the previous activity, it will be an excellent source for a listing of students' own fears.) For example, a remedy for fear of injections might be Medicine Muffins or a treatment for fear of dogs might be a recipe for Hush Puppies. Once each student has named his remedy, have him write a corresponding recipe. If desired, have each student write his recipe on a sheet of pastel construction paper, decorate it like a decorative recipe card, and display it on a bulletin board along with the recipes of his classmates.

Janet Lyon-Cardwell—Gr. 2

Just Plain Fancy

Published by Bantam Books

Just Plain Fancy is a heartwarming story about an Amish girl, her family, and a fancy egg. The egg hatches into a fancy chick that grows into a truly fancy bird. After reading *Just Plain Fancy* to your students, guide them in making beautiful paper peacocks. To make a peacock, begin by gluing two sheets of blue paper together end-to-end, creating an approximately 9" x 23""shape. Use scissors to round the corners of five 2" x 2 1/2" green paper rectangles and five 1" x 1 1/2" purple paper rectangles. Then cut three circles from one-inch black paper squares and cut each black circle in half. Trace the peacock body pattern (page 98) onto purple paper and cut it out; then color the beak area black and draw an eye. Accordion-fold the blue paper, and staple it to resemble a fan. Assemble and glue the remaining pieces to the folded paper to complete the peacock.

Christina Boyd—Librarian
Wilson Elementary
Collinsville, OK

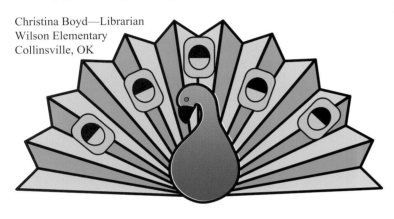

The Bee Tree

Published by Philomel Books

The Bee Tree is based on the experiences of Patricia Polacco's mother, Mary Ellen. It is the story of how her grampa taught her to seek adventure, knowledge, and wisdom between the covers of books. The message is: like a bee, knowledge may be elusive. But if you chase it through the covers of books, it will be yours. Probably many of your students have already begun the chase. So they will be eager to share with their classmates the titles of books that they've encountered along the way.

Make several bee cutouts using the pattern on page 98. Then ask students to name things that they are interested in learning more about. As each topic is called out, label a bee accordingly. Then have students compile lists of books that they've read or located which relate to each of the topics. As they are working, attach an enlarged and colored version of the book pattern on page 98 to a bulletin board. Using a different color of marker for each list, write a twisting loopy trail of titles on the bulletin board, starting at the left side of the board and trailing in the direction of the book cutout. Wherever the trail currently ends, attach the corresponding bee. Encourage youngsters to add new titles to the trails as they are discovered and to use the display as a reference for books they may soon want to read.

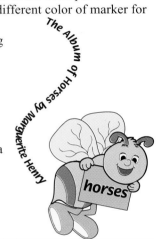

Mrs. Katz And Tush

Published by Bantam Books

In *Mrs. Katz And Tush*, an African-American boy befriends a widowed Jewish lady. This beautiful story is a testament to the value of cross-cultural friendships. One of the expressions that Mrs. Katz uses repeatedly in the story is, "Such a person!"—which is her way of praising someone. After reading the story, ask each child to think of one older friend or relative to feature in this windsock project. Then have him glue a picture or drawing of the person to a tagboard rectangle that has a hole punched near the top, and write "Such A Person!" beneath the picture. Using glue and alphabet-shaped pasta or Alpha-Bits, have him label the back of the tagboard with the name of the person. Then on long strips of different colors of tissue paper, have the child write qualities that make this person "such a person!" Glue the strips to the bottom of the tagboard before suspending the tagboard from the ceiling. Later have each student present his windsock to the person it honors.

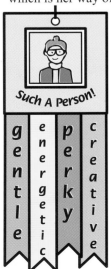

Babushka Baba Yaga

Published by Philomel Books

In *Babushka Baba Yaga*, Polacco reminds us that people are often not what they appear to be. The story encourages readers to look beyond superficial appearances and hearsay and "see" with their hearts. Read *Babushka Baba Yaga* to your youngsters. Then ask them to think of (but not name) someone whom they previously misjudged on the basis of appearances. Encourage them to describe the difference between what the person appeared to be and what she actually was. Have each student glue two heart cutouts to another so that the smaller heart can be flipped up when the glue is dry. Around the smaller heart, have the child write words to describe what the person seemed to be like. Then have him flip up the smaller heart and write words to describe what the person was really like once superficial impressions were set aside. Encourage students to discuss their heart projects but to avoid mentioning names.

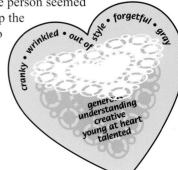

Rechenka's Eggs

Published by Philomel Books

Patricia Polacco's relatives are from the Ukraine and the Georgian provinces in Russia where the delicate art of painting eggs originated. Thanks in part to her *Babushka* (grandmother), who taught her this traditional art, she too is talented in the art of Ukrainian egg painting, called *pysanky*. Egg painting is the subject of the book *Rechenka's Eggs*. Reading Rainbow featured *Rechenka's Eggs* during one of its programs. Following a reading of the story during the program, Patricia Polacco demonstrated the art of egg painting. To acquaint your students with *Rechenka's Eggs* or to extend a reading of the book by introducing students to the author and/or pysanky, play the Reading Rainbow videotape for your students. If a copy is unavailable from your school librarian, call GPN at 1-800-228-4630 to obtain ordering information. (You may also want to inquire about purchasing a copy of the Reading Rainbow program containing Polacco's *Mrs. Katz And Tush*, which was a new Reading Rainbow selection during the fall of 1993.)

Christina Boyd—Librarian
Wilson Elementary
Collinsville, OK

Appelmando's Dreams

Published by Philomel Books

Appelmando's Dreams is a Polacco story that shows how one boy's dreams affect his friends and townsfolk. After reading the story aloud, ask students to define *dreams.* Then find out what they think their dreams would look like, if they could be seen by others. Provide bulletin-board paper and paints, and ask each student to paint one or more of his dreams on the paper. When the dream renderings are dry, display them around the room so that they brighten the classroom much like Appelemando's dreams brightened his village.

Chicken Sunday

Published by Philomel Books

When Patricia was four years old, her grandmother died. Shortly thereafter she and her mom moved to Oakland, California. It was there that she was befriended by an African-American family that included Eula Mae Walker and her grandsons, Stewart and Winston Washington. To this day, Patricia claims Stewart as her best friend. In Patricia's Easter story, *Chicken Sunday*, students can meet Eula Mae, Stewart, Winston, and Patricia. After reading aloud and discussing the story, you may want to show students the portion of the *Rechenka's Eggs* Reading Rainbow program that shows Patricia Polacco making pysanky eggs. (See the previous suggestion for more information.) Then assist your students in making similar egg designs to those in *Chicken Sunday*. To make an egg, have each student design and heavily color an egg-shaped cutout using crayons. Then, using a large brush and watered-down tempera paint, have him cover the entire egg cutout. Or have students create a series of designs on an egg-shaped cutout using glue which has been tinted black with tempera paint. Several days later, when the glue has thoroughly dried, provide watercolor paint sets for students to use to color the areas not covered by glue.

Encourage your students to reexamine *Chicken Sunday*, looking for an actual photograph of the author as a young girl.

adapted from an idea by Cathy Collier
Southeastern Elementary
Chesapeake, VA

Answer Key And Patterns

Use bee and book patterns with *The Bee Tree* on page 96.

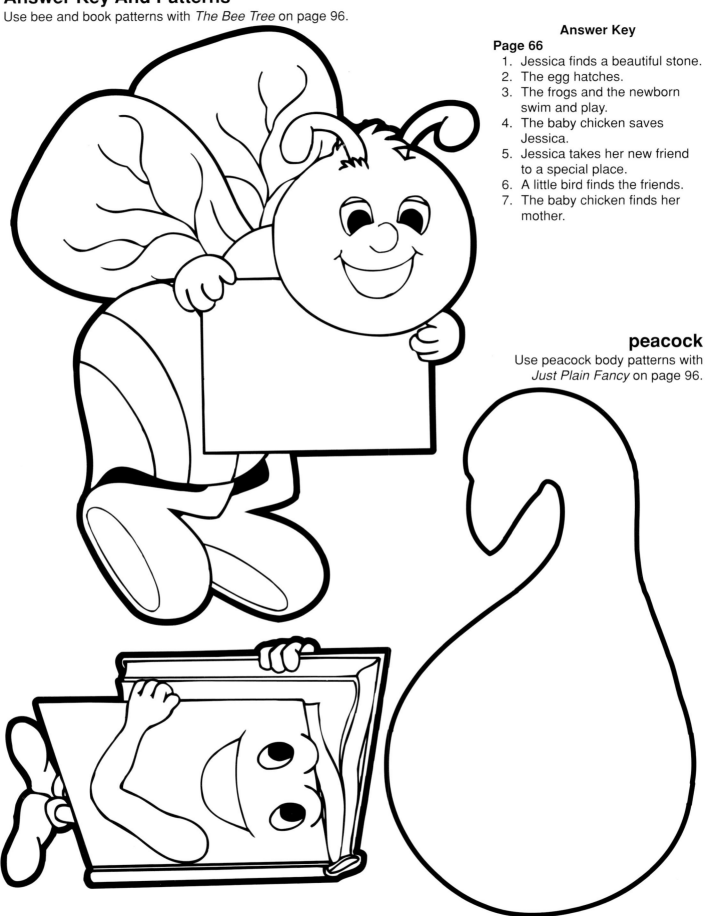

Answer Key

Page 66
1. Jessica finds a beautiful stone.
2. The egg hatches.
3. The frogs and the newborn swim and play.
4. The baby chicken saves Jessica.
5. Jessica takes her new friend to a special place.
6. A little bird finds the friends.
7. The baby chicken finds her mother.

peacock

Use peacock body patterns with *Just Plain Fancy* on page 96.

A Celebration Of
Cynthia Rylant's Books

Cynthia Rylant has captured the attention and hearts of numerous children, teachers, and adults by sharing her gift of writing. The following pages feature a sampling of the author's outstanding books along with several related classroom activities. Let your celebration begin!

Meet The Author

Cynthia Rylant is the award-winning author of more than 60 books for young readers. She has written poetry, novels, an autobiography, and picture books. Most recently she tried her hand at writing *and* illustrating picture books and has found great success. So how did a little girl from West Virginia who grew up *without* books become an award-winning writer? Rylant's straightforward and moving autobiography *But I'll Be Back: An Album* (Orchard Books, 1989) is an intriguing and entertaining look at the author's formative years. Written for readers ages 12 and over, the book is a wonderful resource for teachers of the primary grades.

Today Cynthia Rylant resides in Oregon with her son Nate, two cats (Blueberry and Edward Velvetpaws), and two dogs (Martha and Leia). She professes to being a bit of a homebody who enjoys spending time with her son and arranging, rearranging, and redecorating her home. She also enjoys watching whales, sea otters, and dolphins; viewing films—and writing, of course!

Miss Maggie

Illustrated by Thomas DiGrazia
E. P. Dutton, Inc.; 1983
(This book is out of print. Check your library.)

Nat Crawford's grandmother occasionally sends him to Miss Maggie's house with a gallon of buttermilk or a kettle of beans. But he won't befriend the wrinkled old lady because he's heard about the big black snake that resides in the rafters of her rickety old house. This tenderhearted tale about two very special people who become the best of friends won't soon be forgotten.

Follow up your oral reading of the story by asking students to give reasons why someone might hesitate to get to know another person. List these reasons on the chalkboard. As a class examine the list and look for fallacies in the statements. When the class determines that a reason is invalid, ask a student volunteer to draw a snake outline around the reason. Conclude the activity by discussing a variety of safe ways to initiate new friendships.

Nat's simply decorated cans brought a great deal of pleasure to Miss Maggie. And no doubt empty cans decorated by your students will bring great pleasure to others as well. To decorate a clean can, brush the sides of the can with a layer of thinned glue; then cover the glue with overlapping tissue-paper squares. Brush on another layer of thinned glue and set the can aside to dry. Later embellish the cans with ribbons and other decorations. Students may decide to present the cans to family members and friends. Or they may choose to present their handcrafted treasures to the residents of a local nursing home.

All I See

Illustrated by Peter Catalanotto
Orchard Books, 1988

Day after day a shy boy watches a lakeside painter from afar. And each day when the painter takes a break from his easel and drifts out on the lake in his canoe, the boy sneaks up to view the work of art that is left on display. One day, the canvas is blank, so the shy boy paints a little something for the painter. Soon the two are friends and painting side by side.

Protect your tabletops with newspaper in preparation for this painting activity, or borrow several easels and protect the floor beneath them. Provide paper, brushes, paints, a smock, and lots of space for each student. Play a recording of Beethoven's Fifth Symphony as your youngsters paint quietly or hum along if they wish. Encourage students to paint the things that they "see"—like Gregory did. When each of the paintings is dry, roll it up, tie it with a ribbon, and encourage the artist to give it to a friend or someone whom she'd like to get to know.

The Relatives Came

Illustrated by Stephen Gammell
Bradbury Press, 1985

In this delightful romp, a carload of relatives bump and bounce their way from Virginia to a place on the north side of the mountains where another crowd of relatives is awaiting their summer arrival. The weeks that follow are filled with love, laughter, and lots of food.

When the relatives return to Virginia at the end of the summer, they take with them many pleasant memories and dreams of summers to come. Ask your students to think of unforgettable trips or times that they spent with relatives or family friends. Then have each child write and illustrate a paragraph describing the memorable event. Set aside time for students to share their stories with their classmates.

Amy Scott—Substitute Teacher, Morgantown, WV

It was summer when the relatives arrived, but what if it had been fall, winter, or spring? Write the four seasons of the year on the chalkboard. Ask students to recall how the relatives spent their summer stay in the mountains. List their ideas under the heading of "Summer." Next ask the students how the relatives' stay might have been different if they had arrived during a different season. Then, for each of the three remaining seasons, list your students' ideas for how the relatives might spend their time in the mountains. Use the resulting information to write three more stories about the relatives. If desired, write the stories as a class; then divide the students into three groups and have each group provide the illustrations for a different story. Wouldn't Cynthia Rylant be impressed!

adapted from an idea by Marian Brovero—Gr. 2, Crescent School, Waldwick, NJ

Mr. Griggs' Work

Illustrated by Julie Downing
Orchard Books, 1989

Mr. Griggs is a postman who absolutely loves his work. When he's not working at the post office, he's thinking about being there! Cheery text and illustrations portray the life of a proud and productive postman who is dearly loved by the town he has befriended.

At the conclusion of the book, ask students to recall the different responsibilities that Mr. Griggs has as a postal worker. Also discuss the importance of a postal worker's job. If possible, arrange a field trip to a local post office or invite a postal worker into your classroom to talk about his job.

This story provides the perfect opportunity to explore postage stamps. Remind students that Mr. Griggs thought of a postage stamp every time he saw a chipmunk! Ask students to solicit the help of their parents and others to collect used postage stamps. Place the stamps where students can examine and compare them. Discuss the different looks, shapes, sizes, and values of the collected stamps with your students. Then, as a culminating event, hold a stamp-designing contest. Invite each child to design a stamp on a 9" x 12" sheet of white construction paper. Display the stamp entries on a bulletin board titled "Special Delivery!" and award all entrants for their efforts.

Amy Scott—Substitute Teacher, Morgantown, WV

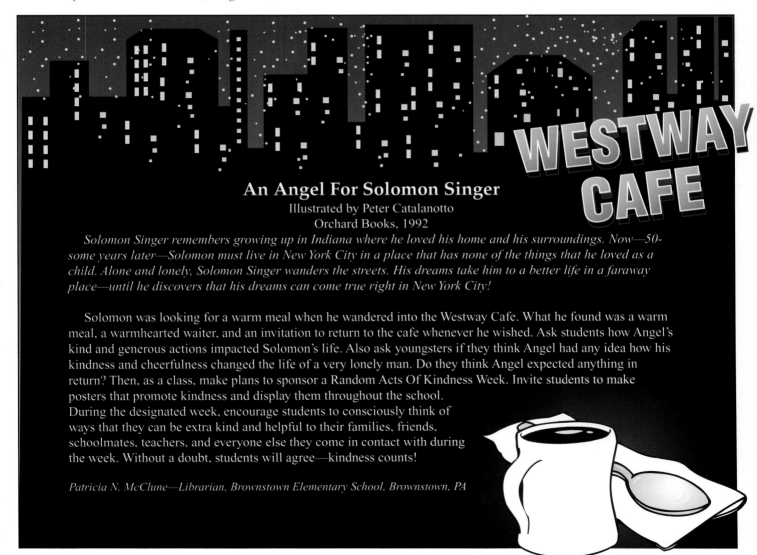

An Angel For Solomon Singer

Illustrated by Peter Catalanotto
Orchard Books, 1992

Solomon Singer remembers growing up in Indiana where he loved his home and his surroundings. Now—50-some years later—Solomon must live in New York City in a place that has none of the things that he loved as a child. Alone and lonely, Solomon Singer wanders the streets. His dreams take him to a better life in a faraway place—until he discovers that his dreams can come true right in New York City!

Solomon was looking for a warm meal when he wandered into the Westway Cafe. What he found was a warm meal, a warmhearted waiter, and an invitation to return to the cafe whenever he wished. Ask students how Angel's kind and generous actions impacted Solomon's life. Also ask youngsters if they think Angel had any idea how his kindness and cheerfulness changed the life of a very lonely man. Do they think Angel expected anything in return? Then, as a class, make plans to sponsor a Random Acts Of Kindness Week. Invite students to make posters that promote kindness and display them throughout the school. During the designated week, encourage students to consciously think of ways that they can be extra kind and helpful to their families, friends, schoolmates, teachers, and everyone else they come in contact with during the week. Without a doubt, students will agree—kindness counts!

Patricia N. McClune—Librarian, Brownstown Elementary School, Brownstown, PA

Dog Heaven

Illustrated by Cynthia Rylant
The Blue Sky Press, 1995

"When dogs go to Heaven, they don't need wings because God knows that dogs love running best." Cynthia Rylant has created what every pet lover has hoped for—a safe haven for their furry friends who have passed away. In Dog Heaven there are open places to run, angel children to play with, and plenty of doggy biscuits. Fluffy clouds make doggy beds, and all dogs—even those who had no real homes on earth—are given homes in Dog Heaven. Any child or adult who has grieved the loss of a beloved pet will find comfort in this playful book.

The inspiration for this book was provided by a friend of the author. The friend was picturing her dog, who had recently died, in a happy place doing the kinds of things it enjoyed the most. Invite students to talk about their pets, past and present. If a child doesn't have a pet, invite him to talk about the pet of a relative, friend, or neighbor. Then ask each child to think of one thing he feels certain his pet (or adopted pet for the day) enjoys doing the most. Have each child describe and illustrate the activity on a sheet of drawing paper. Bind the projects into a class collection called "Favorite Pet Pastimes." Place the book in your classroom library for further reading enjoyment.

My dog likes to catch a Frisbee.

Donna Kester Phillips, Grand Island, NY

For another delightful dog tale, read aloud Rylant's *The Bookshop Dog* (The Blue Sky Press, 1996). Everyone who comes to Martha Jane's Bookshop comes to see Martha Jane, the bookshop owner's dog. The townsfolk love the pooch so much that when the bookshop owner needs an operation, they begin to argue about who should take care of Martha Jane. But Martha Jane has a mind of her own and chooses her own caretaker—and what a dandy choice it turns out to be!

The Old Woman Who Named Things

Illustrated by Kathryn Brown
Harcourt Brace & Company, 1996

Tired of the loneliness that resulted from outliving all her friends, an inventive old woman comes up with a plan. She will only give names to the things that she's certain will outlast her—like "Fred" her chair, "Roxanne" her bed, and "Betsy" her car. But her plan is put to the test when a shy, brown dog, who has won her heart, is missing. After a valiant search for the dog, she enlists the help of the local dogcatcher, who asks, "What's the dog's name?"

Although the premise of this story may be a bit sophisticated for younger children, they are sure to delight in its happy ending. Find out how many students have helped name pets and younger siblings. Next ask the youngsters to share their strategies for picking a perfect name. After writing their ideas and a few of your own on the chalkboard, inform students that one more name needs to be chosen. When the youngsters realize that the old lady herself is nameless, have the students recall what they know about the woman. Then page through the book so that the students can study the illustrations of the old lady sporting her cowboy boots, lavender glasses, and beehive hairdo. Write the students' name suggestions on the chalkboard; then hold a class vote to determine the perfect name for the old lady. Of course, an old lady this unique could very easily have quite a lengthy name!

Robert D. San Souci
A Master Storyteller

In a world in which far too many things seem mundane, mass-produced, and sacrificed for the bottom line, Robert D. San Souci refuses to compromise. He infuses his work with knowledge, passion, respect, and painstaking care—making him a master at his trade. On the following pages, you'll find introductions to several of San Souci's works and related classroom activities.

contributions by Donna C. Kester Phillips

About The Author

Robert D. San Souci is best known for his vivid retellings of folktales from around the world. His meticulous attention to the history of a story, his sensitivity to a story's cultural roots, and his awareness of his readers' needs guide him in his work. Inspired and encouraged by his parents and teachers, he at one time trained to become a teacher; but circumstances led him instead to take up work as a bookseller, an advertising copywriter, an editor, and—lucky for us—a writer!

San Souci's life in sunny California and his family have played an important part in his work. His parents were inveterate readers who loved to read books aloud. He had a grandmother who "may have forgotten a piece of luggage when she came to visit, but never forgot a good book." From these loved ones he gained a respect and a love for literature. His early interest in storytelling and writing was also reinforced by his brother Daniel's lifelong interest in book illustration. The brothers (who share the same October 10 birth date, though Robert is two years older) published their first book, *The Legend Of Scarface*, together in 1978. Since then they have collaborated on several other books, including *Song Of Sedna, The Christmas Ark,* and *Feathertop.*

While San Souci tries his hand at adult fantasy books and nonfiction, writes for several magazines published by Cobblestone Press, and serves as a story consultant to Walt Disney Feature Animation Studios, his first love remains the children's picture book. The pleasure of retelling traditional tales for a new audience has led to such favorite books as *The Talking Eggs, Sootface, Sukey And The Mermaid,* and *The Faithful Friend.* When pressed to name a character in his books he most identifies with, the author suggests "Scarface, who is decent and shy, not exactly a hero, but willing to do the best he can when the need is there."

The author's ideas for his books come from extensive library research (at last count he had cards to some 28 different libraries), from his travels, and from his "Weird File" of unusual newspaper clippings and notes collected over the years. The author believes you are never too old or too young to become published, knowing both a 70-year-old and a second grader who have just "arrived." His advice to budding writers is "not to be discouraged" at rejection, "to get to work on a new project as soon as one is completed," and "to recognize that what sets the writer apart from the wanna-be is *perseverance.*"

Writing To The Author

Robert San Souci welcomes mail from teachers and children. As a courtesy to the author, it's best to send either one letter from the class or to package individual student letters in a single large envelope. These can be sent to the author's mailing address:

Robert D. San Souci
2261 Market Street, Box 503
San Francisco, CA 94114

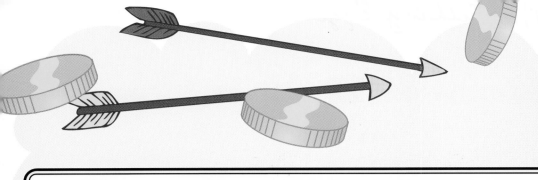

The Legend Of Scarface: A Blackfeet Indian Tale
Illustrated by Daniel San Souci
Bantam Doubleday Dell Books For Young Readers, 1978

Scarface—a young Native American so named for the birthmark on his cheek—is in love with the chief's beautiful daughter. Because he is neither rich nor handsome, he is taunted by his peers. But the chief's daughter sees Scarface for who he is—an honest man with a generous heart. When the young man learns that his beloved has vowed to Father Sun that she will never marry, Scarface makes the treacherous journey to the land of the Sun. Now he must find the courage to ask Father Sun—the father of all—to release the chief's daughter from her vow.

At the conclusion of the story, write the words "kindness," "bravery," and "honesty" on the chalkboard. Ask students to describe how each of these traits enable Scarface to earn the love of the chief's daughter, the friendship of the forest animals, and the blessing of Father Sun. Then write the word "trust" on the chalkboard and find out how students think this trait relates to Scarface's story. Next ask students to compare themselves to Scarface. To do this have each child copy and complete each of the following sentences on a sheet of paper: "I think Scarface and I are alike because...", "One way I'd like to be more like Scarface is...", and "I think one thing Scarface would like most about me is...." Before you collect these papers, invite each child to read aloud one or more of his sentences. Students are sure to be pleased to learn that the author, Robert D. San Souci, has compared himself to Scarface, too! (See "About The Author" on page 103.)

Song Of Sedna
Illustrated by Daniel San Souci
Bantam Doubleday Dell Books For Young Readers, 1981

This ancient Eskimo legend tells the story of a beautiful maiden, Sedna, who is courted by men from near and far. But Sedna only wishes to marry the handsome hunter whom she has often seen in her dreams. In time the hunter comes and the two are married, but all is not as it appears. Mattak, Sedna's new husband, has a hidden identity—one that terrifies Sedna. This compelling rendition of how an Eskimo maiden became the goddess of the sea is powerful and haunting.

When Sedna became the goddess of the sea, she learned that anything she wished for was within her power, and that she should be wise and merciful with her wishes. Encourage students to explain how Sedna's actions proved that she was worthy of being goddess of the sea. Then, after a second oral reading of the story, enlist your students' help in recalling events from the story. Write the events on the chalkboard. On 12" x 18" sheets of drawing paper, ask each student or student pair to illustrate a different story event. With your students' help, sequence the projects in story order. Then bind the projects between two 12" x 18" sheets of light blue construction paper. On the front cover, write "Song Of Sedna" and "Retold By The Students In Room ____." In turn let each child illustrate a different sea creature on the booklet's front or back cover. Then gather the students together for a retelling of Sedna's story. Place the booklet on an easel. Each time you turn to a different booklet page, the illustrator(s) of that page tell the corresponding part of the story.

The Enchanted Tapestry

Illustrated by László Gál

Dial Books For Young Readers, 1987

Based on an ancient Chinese folktale, this elegantly told story is one of mystery and majesty. At the heart of the story is a poor widow who weaves beautiful silk tapestries. One day a strong wind suddenly tears her most precious tapestry from its frame and whirls it away. The grief-stricken widow immediately falls ill. Knowing that only the return of the weaving will bring back their mother's will to live, each of her three sons searches for the tapestry. However, only the youngest son is willing to endanger his life to retrieve the beautiful weaving. This young lad's love and courage result in a dream come true for himself and his mother.

The widow's tapestry was a detailed picture of her hopes and dreams. Remind students that the widow had been working on the tapestry for more than one year, working by sunlight and candlelight. Ask students to explain what this tells them about the value of the weaving.

Inform students that you'd like them to create a classroom tapestry that pictures their hopes and dreams for the future. To prepare for this, secure a large sheet of white paper to a tabletop and use a pencil to visually divide the paper into sections—one per student. Each student takes a turn illustrating his hopes and dreams for the future in one section of the paper. When each child has completed his illustration, carefully remove the large-size artwork from the tabletop, trim it as needed, and display it in a school hallway or the library for others to see. Perhaps this tapestry is enchanted, too!

The Talking Eggs

Illustrated by Jerry Pinkney

Dial Books For Young Readers, 1989

Adapted from a Creole folktale, this imaginative story takes youngsters to a wondrous world in which inner beauty hides ugliness, and plain objects conceal great treasures. Hearts will be stolen by kindhearted Blanche and resentments stirred up by Rose, her self-centered sister. And in the end, the old wise woman will be applauded for the manner in which she uses her talking eggs to reward the actions of each girl.

Each sister helps determine her fate by the decisions she makes. Blanche, who respects the old woman's requests, is rewarded with riches. Rose, who favors her own desires, remains poor and unhappy. Invite students to tell about choices (wise or unwise) that they have made and share the consequences of their actions.

Then egg on your youngsters' creativity with this writing activity! First have students recall how Blanche received her lovely gifts. Next ask each child to choose the gift she would like to have spill out from a magical egg. On the count of three, have each student pretend to toss an egg over her left shoulder. Then, on egg-shaped writing paper, have each student describe the gift that spilled out and tell how that gift might change her life. Invite students to read their stories aloud. Then bind the student stories between egg-shaped construction-paper covers. Title the class booklet " 'Egg-normous' Wishes," and place it in the classroom library for all to enjoy.

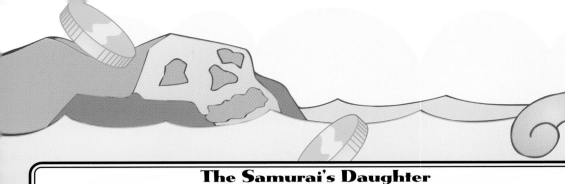

The Samurai's Daughter

Illustrated by Stephen T. Johnson

Dial Books For Young Readers, 1992

In this thrilling retelling of a Japanese legend, a samurai nobleman is sent into exile on a lonely island in a distant sea. His determined young daughter—who is as strong and brave as any samurai—pledges to join her father. Throughout her journey she encounters many terrors and trials, the most dangerous of which is a monstrous sea serpent. How the daughter meets each challenge and is finally reunited with her beloved father creates an electrifying tale that youngsters are sure to enjoy.

When word spread of what the samurai's brave daughter had done, the family was given many honors. Ask students to recall the honorable qualities of each character. Next ask each student to make a list of her honorable qualities. Remind students that while they may share some qualities with the samurai and his daughter, they will probably have different honorable qualities, too. For a fun writing follow-up, have each student study his list of qualities, then write and illustrate a story in which he uses his honorable qualities to rescue his parent(s) or a friend!

The Boy And The Ghost

Illustrated by Brian Pinkney

Simon And Schuster Books For Young Readers, 1989

Kindness, courage, and honesty reap grand rewards in this American folktale adaptation. Thomas (the boy) decides to lend his hardworking parents a hand and sets out for the city to earn extra money for them and his six siblings. Along the way Thomas helps a stranger. The grateful stranger directs Thomas to a huge house where a treasure is hidden—and guarded by a fearsome ghost! If Thomas can remain in the house from sundown to sunup, the treasure and the house will be his.

"Boo-tiful" Behavior Pays Off!

Thomas earns a pot of gold and a house by being a brave, honest, and well-mannered boy. Take a class poll to find out if students think the red-haired ghost with fingers that blazed like a torch was scary. Then, using a similar story plot, challenge each student to write and illustrate a ghost story. As a prewriting activity, have each student identify where he is going, what he hopes to find, who will tell him about a ghost, how he outsmarts the ghost, and what he does with his reward. When the stories are written and illustrated, invite students to share their work with their classmates.

Here's a positive discipline strategy that's sure to interest your youngsters! From brown paper cut out a large pot that resembles the earthen pot pictured in the story. Attach the cutout to a bulletin board along with a paper ghost and the title " 'Boo-tiful' Behavior Pays Off!" Then cut out a predetermined number of yellow construction-paper coins and keep them handy. Each time you observe your students displaying exceptional manners, acts of kindness, or other desirable traits and actions, staple a paper coin in or near the pot. When all the paper coins have been stapled to the display, reward your class with a special privilege.

Sukey And The Mermaid
Illustrated by Brian Pinkney
Simon And Schuster Books For Young Readers, 1992

"Storyteller say, this happened oncet upon a time, on a little island off the coast of South Carolina." And so begins this story of Sukey, a poor, unhappy girl who lives with her ma and new step-pa. One day, to escape her step-pa's bossy ways, Sukey runs away to her secret hiding place by the sea. Here a mermaid answers her cries for help and eventually takes her below the sea to a gentle place without time or pain. But after a while, Sukey pines for the real world. In the end, Sukey's wishes are answered—but not by treasure or the sea's magic. Instead it is goodness and love and her own inner strength that, at long last, bring joy to Sukey's heart.

At the conclusion of the story, ask students why they think Sukey longed to go back to the real world. What did she miss? Then have students brainstorm the pros and cons of living permanently under the sea. List their ideas on the chalkboard in two columns. Allow time for students to evaluate the lists of information; then encourage students to explain the choices they might have made had they been Sukey. Next ask students if they think Sukey and Dembo could have found happiness without the mermaid's treasure. Find out why they think the mermaid returned the treasure to the beach and what they think Sukey and Dembo will do with it. Then, on a sheet of story paper, have each youngster illustrate herself talking to a mermaid and write what they are chatting about.

Sootface: An Ojibwa Cinderella Story
Illustrated by Daniel San Souci
Bantam Doubleday Dell Books For Young Readers, 1994

Once an Ojibwa man—after the death of his wife—raised his three daughters alone. The two older girls were lazy and irritable. The youngest daughter—who was called Sootface by her sisters—was forced to do most of the work. While Sootface worked she dreamed that she might one day find a husband. But how could she, an unkept girl, ever be so lucky?

I plan to nurture my inner beauty by:

• reading more poetry

• spending time in a garden

• listening to music

• fishing

• playing with my younger brother

Before reading *Sootface* to your youngsters, ask them to tell you the story of Cinderella. As they mention different elements of the story, note them on the chalkboard in a column beneath the title "Cinderella." Read aloud *Sootface* and discuss the story as a class. Ask students to name elements of the story that parallel elements from their telling. What explanations do youngsters have for the differences between the two tales? Revisit the book, taking time to study the radiant illustrations that convey the natural woodland setting and give readers a glimpse into the life the Ojibwa once lived. Discuss with students how the story elements in *Sootface* are tied to that culture. Point out that in all Cinderella stories, it is inner beauty that prevails over evil. For an interesting writing activity, ask each child to list five ways he plans to nurture his inner beauty.

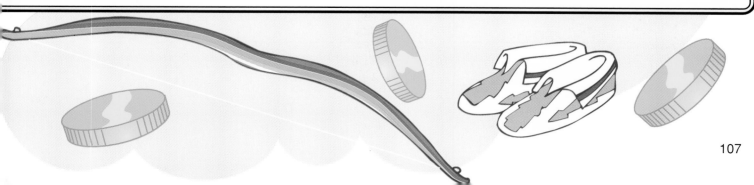

The House In The Sky: A Bahamian Folktale
Illustrated by Wil Clay
Dial Books For Young Readers, 1996

The value of honest work is emphasized in this entertaining retelling of Caribbean folklore. Two lazy brothers—one clever and one not-so-clever—journey deep into the jungle to steal food from the sky house. The clever brother fills his sack and quickly leaves. But the not-so-clever brother—who is also greedy—decides to gorge himself first, then fill his bag. The resulting romp teaches the lazy brothers that the best way to provide food for their families is to grow their own!

There's little doubt that your youngsters will want to hear this fun-filled, action-packed retelling again and again! After several oral readings of the story, ask each student to write the story title and illustrate the house in the sky on one side of an oaktag semicircle, then write his name on the other side. Next have each student choose two, three, or four favorite parts of the story and illustrate each one on a different construction-paper rectangle. On the back of each illustration, have the student write a brief description of the pictured event. To assemble his project, a student punches one hole in the top of each rectangle and a matching number of evenly spaced holes along the bottom of his semicircle. He also punches one hole at the top of the semicircle. Using lengths of yarn or string, he suspends the rectangles from the bottom of the semicircle. He also attaches a length of yarn or string to the top of the semicircle for suspending the project. Display the completed mobiles in your media center to create added interest in this super piece of storytelling.

The Faithful Friend
Illustrated by Brian Pinkney
Simon And Schuster Books For Young Readers, 1995

On the lush Caribbean island of Martinique in the 19th century, two young men—who are best friends—set out to meet a young woman whom one of the men has fallen hopelessly in love with. At their destination they encounter the woman's frightening, wizardlike uncle. Determined to not let his niece marry the young man whom she has also fallen in love with, the uncle plots to destroy the couple before a wedding can take place. Only the young man's faithful friend can save the lovers. The result is an extraordinary tale of romance, intrigue, and incomparable courage in which the truest of friends remain faithful to the very end.

Follow up this story by asking students to brainstorm characteristics that they feel are important for their friends to have. Write the students' ideas on the chalkboard and encourage group discussion. Then, under your students' direction, underline the characteristics belonging to Clement and Hippolyte, the friends in the story.

This writing activity encourages students to reflect on their friendships. Give each student a booklet of blank pages. Each day ask a friendship-related question such as "What do you like to do with friends?" or, "Why do you think that you are a good friend to have?" You could also have students answer friendship-related questions about the story. When the booklets are filled, have students title and decorate their booklet covers to their liking.

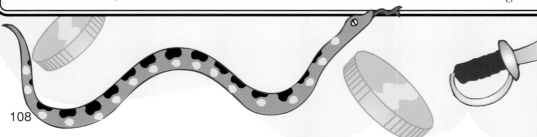

Math + Poetry = Shel Silverstein

Shel Silverstein's outrageous poems add up to countless opportunities for teaching math-related skills! Watch the enthusiasm of your youngsters multiply as they giggle their way through the following poems and math activities. The only way to sum it up is *total* fun!

ideas by Lisa Leonardi

A Light In The Attic

HarperCollins Children's Books, 1981

The poems reviewed on pages 109 and 110—"Snake Problem," "Overdues," and "Homework Machine"—are from *A Light In The Attic* by Shel Silverstein.

"Snake Problem"

What do you do when a 24-foot python says, "I love you"? That's the lengthy dilemma facing the child in this love poem.

A 24-foot python is the perfect tool to help your students inch their way toward better measurement skills! After several oral readings of the poem, have each student draw and color a snake on a provided card, then write his name on the card for easy identification. Before asking students to estimate the distance of 24 feet, show them a one-foot paper snake (or a ruler) as a frame of reference. Then lead students into the hallway. On a wall designate the end of an imaginary 24-foot python. Instruct each student to tape his snake card to the wall where he thinks the python's head would be if the snake stretched out to its full 24-foot length. To check the accuracy of your students' estimates, tape a 24-foot length of yarn along the wall. Wow! What a snake!

Students will slither their way to better nonstandard measurement skills with this partner activity! Give each pair of students a one-foot construction-paper python, a pencil, paper, and a variety of manipulatives such as Unifix® cubes, paper clips, craft sticks, and cotton swabs. Have partners measure the length of their python using each type of manipulative and record their findings on the paper as shown. To conclude the activity, have student pairs compare their findings. For older students, multiply the fun by asking them to calculate the number of manipulatives needed to create snakes of various lengths. For example, "If ten small paper clips are needed to make a one-foot python, how many paper clips are needed to make a five-foot snake?"

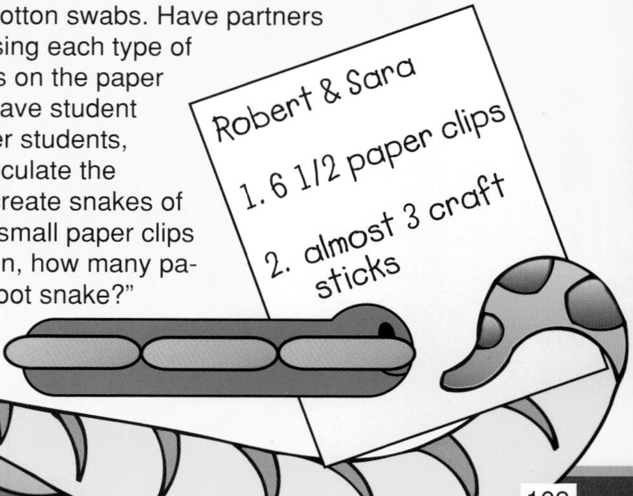

Robert & Sara

1. 6 1/2 paper clips

2. almost 3 craft sticks

"Homework Machine"

The Homework Machine would be the most perfect contraption if only nine plus four equaled three!

Students will be eager to teach this homework machine a thing or two about basic math facts! Copy the poem on chart paper and display it in a prominent classroom location. As you read the poem aloud, have students follow along or read aloud with you. Then enlist your students' help in fixing the homework machine! To begin the repair, tape a blank card over the word *not* (in the next-to-last line of the poem) so that instead of being a not-so-perfect homework contraption, it becomes a perfect one! Also tape a laminated card over each of the two sums, and a laminated sentence strip (or something similar) over the math fact. Next use a wipe-off marker to program each laminated card with the same sum. Challenge students to write on their papers addition sentences that equal the posted sum. After several minutes invite the students to share the sentences they created. Be sure to try out a few of the sentences in the poem. To do this, use your wipe-off marker to program the sentence strip with the desired number sentence. After the poem has been recited, wipe away the number sentence and the strip is ready to reprogram for another oral reading.

For a daily kid-pleasing math challenge, keep the poem on display. Each day reprogram the two laminated cards with a desired numeral and challenge students to write a designated number of math sentences (addition, subtraction, and/or multiplication) that equal the posted numeral. This homework machine works like a charm!

"Overdues"

A library book is found that is long overdue—42 years, to be exact! The question remains whether to return the book or hide it again.

After a few oral readings of "Overdues," this book-related activity is sure to make "cents" at your math center! Check out several books from your school library. Insert an overdue notice with a different fine inside the pocket of each library book. Place the books and a large supply of plastic or paper coins at a center. A student selects a book and uses the coins to pay the fine. Either check students' work or provide a self-checking answer key that lists the possible coin combinations for each fine.

Further challenge students with this large-group activity. Assign a fine, such as five cents, for each day a book is late. Then, using a variety of books, announce a number of days that each book is overdue. Students calculate each book's fine on their papers. Vary the daily fine and the number of overdue days until your youngsters have "fine-ly" paid their dues!

Where The Sidewalk Ends

HarperCollins Children's Books, 1974

The poems reviewed on this page—"Smart," "The Googies Are Coming," and "Band-Aids"—are from *Where The Sidewalk Ends* by Shel Silverstein.

"Smart"

Through a series of trades, a boy takes pride in the fact that after starting off with only a single dollar bill, he ends up with five pennies. And five is more than one, isn't it?

This poem provides the perfect opportunity to teach youngsters that more can be less when it comes to coins! Project a transparency like the one shown from an overhead projector. During a second reading of the poem, stop after the first stanza and have a student volunteer place transparent coins on the overhead to show the boy's first money trade. Then enlist the class's help in determining the amount of money lost during the transaction and record this amount in the third column. Repeat this activity after the second, third, and fourth stanzas. After reading the fifth and final stanza, have students calculate the total amount of money the young boy lost. Older students can complete a similar activity on paper. No doubt your students will feel quite *smart* after completing this coin-trading activity!

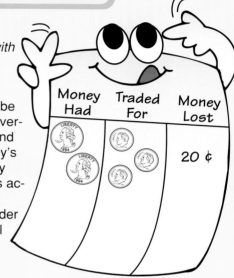

Money Had	Traded For	Money Lost
		20 ¢

"The Googies Are Coming"

The googies buy children of all different shapes and sizes, and at all different prices. They'll pay 15¢ for dirty ones, 30¢ for clean ones, and only a penny for noisy ones! What a bargain!

Happy Ones = 40 ¢

After several readings of this money-filled poem, post individual sentence strips showing the price of each type of child the googies want to buy. With your students' help, arrange the strips in descending order based on the prices. Then use the resulting list to enhance your students' problem-solving skills. To do this, give each child a construction-paper booklet of blank paper. Instruct each child to write her name and the poem title on the front cover, then illustrate what she thinks a googie might look like on the back cover. Each morning display a word problem based on the posted list and challenge students to solve the problem in their booklets before the end of the school day. Then, before dismissal, set aside time for the students to compare their solutions with their classmates and make any necessary adjustments. As an added challenge, invite students to submit to you googie-related problems (with answers) for their classmates to solve.

"Band-Aids"

No need to feel sorry for this boy who's bandaged from head to toe! He doesn't have a cut or even a scratch!

This addition activity is just what the doctor ordered! Copy the poem on the chalkboard. To begin, read the poem aloud and have your students determine how many bandages are on the boy's body. Then erase each number word in the poem and replace it with a blank. Have each child use her best penmanship to copy the poem on handwriting paper, inserting a number word from one to five in each blank. Next ask each student to tally the number of bandages the boy is wearing in her version of the poem, and write this number in the lower right-hand corner of her paper. Finally pair students and have each student check her partner's work. Encourage partners to work together to make any needed corrections. Conclude the activity by attaching a colorful bandage to the back of each child's hand or to her work.

Falling Up

HarperCollins Children's Books, 1996

The poems reviewed on this page—"The Monkey" and "Keepin' Count"—are from *Falling Up* by Shel Silverstein.

"The Monkey"

1 monkey who visited a banana 3 (tree) on his way 2 the store got a stomachache from 7 green bananas that he 8. Silverstein's clever substitution of numbers for words makes this poem a delight 4 youngsters 2 read!

Students will go bananas as they try to decipher this intriguing poem! Before sharing the poem with your students, copy it onto chart paper. Cover each numeral with a card that you've labeled with a number sentence that equals the concealed numeral. As you read the poem aloud, have students solve each number sentence and supply the missing numeral. Then, for a fun follow-up, have each student use the same style of writing to pen a sentence for a classmate to read. Your youngsters are cer10 2 have a gr8 time!

"Keepin' Count"

A student is determined to find out how many flies are in Professor Bacar's jar. He counts to three million and seven, but when a fly lady has a fly baby, he has to start counting again!

You can count on students going buggy over this estimation activity! Purchase a bag of plastic flies and a few plastic spiders from a party shop or the Oriental Trading Company (1-800-228-2269). Put the flies in a clear jar (with a lid) and display the jar in a prominent classroom location. Also post a recording chart similar to the one shown. After an oral reading of the poem, ask each student to estimate the number of flies in the displayed jar. Record each student's estimate on the chart; then enlist the students' help in counting the flies. Write this number on the chart too. Return the flies to the jar and use a permanent marker to draw a line around the jar that shows where the flies stop. Then drop a few spiders in the jar and secure the lid. Remind students that spiders eat flies!

After the students have left for the day, remove a noticeable amount of flies from the jar. The following school day, have the youngsters repeat the estimating and counting activities. Encourage the students to study the jar and refer to the chart so they can use the information that they previously gathered. Repeat the activities two or three more times—on different days—until all the flies have been removed from the jar. Not only will your students have polished their estimation and counting skills—they'll also have learned a thing or two about the food chain!

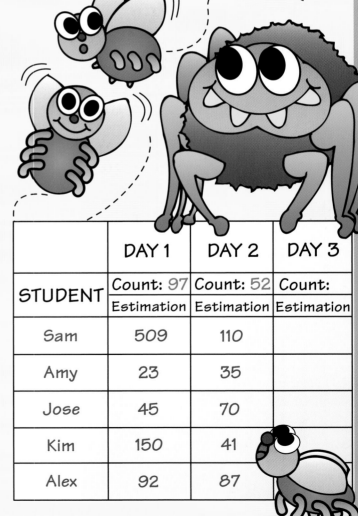

STUDENT	DAY 1 Count: 97	DAY 2 Count: 52	DAY 3 Count:
	Estimation	Estimation	Estimation
Sam	509	110	
Amy	23	35	
Jose	45	70	
Kim	150	41	
Alex	92	87	

A Treasury Of
Chris Van Allsburg
Collectibles

Extraordinary and exquisite. Beautiful and bizarre. Unique and unusual. Strong and surreal. The works of author and illustrator Chris Van Allsburg are all of these and much more. Select from the following books and ideas to introduce your youngsters to the unique style and timeless appeal of Chris Van Allsburg's books.

Jumanji
(Houghton Mifflin Company, 1981)
The game under the tree looked like many others Peter and Judy had at home. Little did they know that when they unfolded its ordinary playing board they would be in for the most exciting and bizarre adventure of their lives.

At Home Alone

Ask your youngsters what they think are the most exciting aspects of staying at home alone (or with older siblings or baby-sitters). Then have each student write and illustrate a story about his most memorable "at-home-alone" experience.

Jumanji Strikes Again

For a fun follow-up writing activity, challenge each of your youngsters to write and illustrate a sequel to Van Allsburg's delightful story. Before students begin to create, reread the final page of *Jumanji* and discuss the habits of the Budwing brothers. Find out what your youngsters think might happen when these two boys begin to play Jumanji. Also ask your youngsters what Mrs. Budwing might find when she returns home. Your youngsters are sure to be filled with ideas when they embark on this writing assignment!

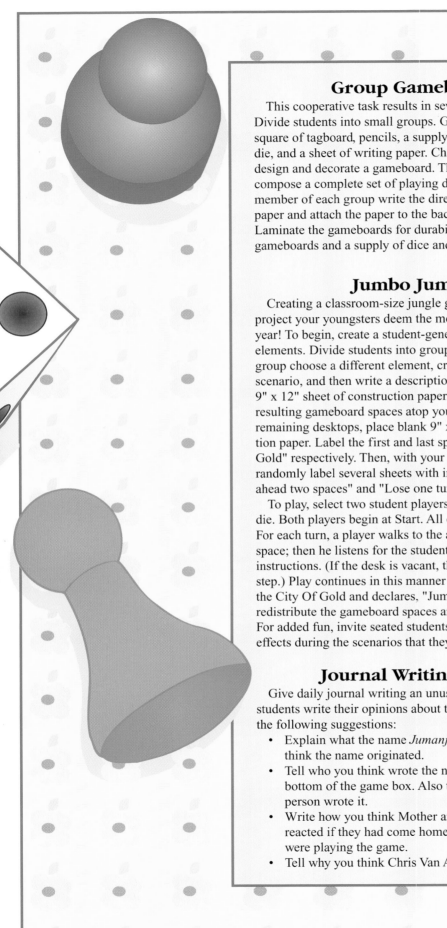

Group Gameboards

This cooperative task results in several jungle gameboards. Divide students into small groups. Give each group a large square of tagboard, pencils, a supply of markers or crayons, a die, and a sheet of writing paper. Challenge each group to design and decorate a gameboard. Then have each group compose a complete set of playing directions. Have one member of each group write the directions on the writing paper and attach the paper to the back of the gameboard. Laminate the gameboards for durability if desired. Store the gameboards and a supply of dice and pawns at a center.

Jumbo Jumanji

Creating a classroom-size jungle gameboard may be the project your youngsters deem the most memorable of the past year! To begin, create a student-generated list of jungle elements. Divide students into groups of three. Have each group choose a different element, create a related gameboard scenario, and then write a description of the scenario on a 9" x 12" sheet of construction paper. Randomly place the resulting gameboard spaces atop your students' desks. On the remaining desktops, place blank 9" x 12" sheets of construction paper. Label the first and last spaces "Start" and "City Of Gold" respectively. Then, with your youngsters' input, randomly label several sheets with instructions such as "Go ahead two spaces" and "Lose one turn."

To play, select two student players and one student to roll a die. Both players begin at Start. All other students are seated. For each turn, a player walks to the appropriate gameboard space; then he listens for the student seated there to read his instructions. (If the desk is vacant, the player completes this step.) Play continues in this manner until one player reaches the City Of Gold and declares, "Jumanji!" To play again, redistribute the gameboard spaces and choose new players. For added fun, invite seated students to perform sound effects during the scenarios that they created.

Journal Writing Topics

Give daily journal writing an unusual twist by having students write their opinions about the story. If desired, use the following suggestions:
- Explain what the name *Jumanji* means and where you think the name originated.
- Tell who you think wrote the note that was taped to the bottom of the game box. Also tell why you think that person wrote it.
- Write how you think Mother and Father would have reacted if they had come home while Peter and Judy were playing the game.
- Tell why you think Chris Van Allsburg wrote this book.

The Stranger

(Houghton Mifflin Company, 1986)
This delightfully mysterious tale is filled with clues, but no solution. It is late summer when Farmer Bailey accidentally hits a man with his truck. The strange man can remember nothing after the accident, so Farmer Bailey takes him to his home to recuperate.

A Key Clue

Clarify a key clue from the story with this simple demonstration. In advance, cut out two matching leaf shapes: one from green construction paper and one from orange construction paper. Glue one cutout atop the other, aligning the edges. Keep the cutout concealed as you begin your story presentation. After the stranger plucks the green leaf from the tree and blows on it with all of his might, reveal the green side of the leaf cutout. Next ask a student to blow on the cutout just as the stranger had blown on the leaf. At this point, slowly turn the cutout so that the orange side can be seen by your youngsters. Who was that stranger, anyway?

The Wreck Of The Zephyr

(Houghton Mifflin Company, 1983)
In this intriguing tale, an old man recounts a young boy's sailing adventure.

Sailing Scenes

Have your youngsters man the sails during this follow-up activity! Give each youngster a large sailboat pattern and a length of white bulletin board paper. First have each student color and cut out his sailboat. Then instruct each youngster to mount his cutout atop his larger paper (however he desires) and create a colorful sailboat scene. Invite students to share their completed projects with their classmates.

Just A Dream

(Houghton Mifflin Company, 1990)
A frightful look at the future convinces a young boy to do everything that he can to preserve the earth's environment.

Cooperative Issues

Increase your youngsters' environmental awareness by using this cooperative learning project. Divide students into small groups; then have each group choose a different dream episode from the story. Have each group discuss reasons why its episode occurred and how this situation might have been prevented. Then have each group design an awareness poster about its particular environmental issue.

The Mysteries Of Harris Burdick
(Houghton Mifflin Company, 1984)
Unsolved mysteries lurk within the covers of this unique picture book. And the solution to each one is not found in the book, but instead in one's own imagination.

Creative Interpretations

Using the information found in the book's preface, share the strange disappearance of Harris Burdick and the mystery of his drawings. Then examine each picture carefully and discuss its title and caption. During the next few weeks, present the pictures as topics for creative writing. Have students write stories independently, with partners, in small groups, or as a large group. Or have students give oral story presentations. Whatever you choose, you can count on a wealth of student creativity!

The Garden Of Abdul Gasazi
(Houghton Mifflin Company, 1979)
The sign read: "Absolutely, positively no dogs allowed in this garden. At the bottom it was signed: Abdul Gasazi, retired magician." So when the dog Alan is caring for escapes into the garden, Alan races after it. Can he save the dog from the magician's magical spell?

Maze Makers

This follow-up activity is "a-maze-ingly" fun! First have each student create a garden maze. To do this, a student draws Alan in the top left-hand corner of a sheet of drawing paper. Then he draws Fritz the dog in the lower right-hand corner. He then draws a series of garden passageways from Alan to Fritz, making certain that only one of the passageways actually connects the two. When the mazes are complete, pair students and have each student complete his partner's puzzle.

The Garden Of Whom?

You'll have gardens galore when this writing activity is completed. After reading the story aloud, invite each young-ster to write and illustrate a story that tells about his own magical garden.

In my garden all of the plants can talk to me. One day, they told me a secret.

Two Bad Ants

(Houghton Mifflin Company, 1988)
A dangerous adventure teaches two tiny ants a valuable lesson about their home and family.

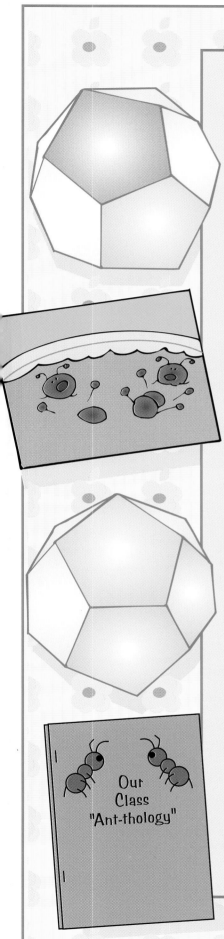

Aspiring Authors

Once students have heard and discussed the tale of the two bad ants, they'll be ready to create their own "bad" tales. Have each youngster entitle his story *Two Bad _____*. Encourage students to write from the perspectives of their chosen characters, just as Chris Van Allsburg has done. Then have each youngster illustrate his story and, if he desires, share it with his classmates.

Keeping The Perspective

For a fun first reading of the story, read aloud the text without revealing any of Van Allsburg's delightful illustrations. At the completion of the story, give each youngster a sheet of drawing paper. Have each student pretend that he is an ant in the story and draw a picture of one thing that he saw. When the drawings are completed, reread the story and invite your youngsters to share their pictures at the appropriate times during the story. Finally share the story again by displaying only Van Allsburg's illustrations.

Those Ants!

Those ants are at it again! Tell your youngsters that the two bad ants are ready for another adventure. Ask your youngsters where the ants should visit; then write their ideas on the chalkboard. Next have each youngster write and illustrate a story about the ants' next adventure. Challenge each student to write and draw from the perspective of an ant.

The ants struggled upward. Their legs felt weak. Then they reached the ledge. The white powder along the ledge stuck to the ants' feet.

Dear Ants,...

For a fun letter-writing activity, have each student write a letter to the two bad ants. Invite students to write a variety of messages in their letters. For instance, a student may congratulate the ants for returning to their home, give them precautionary measures about other dangers that lie outside their home, or give them instructions on how to take another safe, yet exciting, adventure. Write on!

A Class "Ant-thology"

Create an unusual collection of "antwork"! Challenge each youngster to illustrate an ant in a very perplexing predicament. When his illustration is complete, have him write a story about his artwork. Each youngster's story must tell where his ant is, how it got there, and how it will get out. Bind the stories and illustrations in a class booklet entitled *Our Class "Ant-thology."*

The Z Was Zapped

(Houghton Mifflin Company, 1987)
This alphabet book stretches one's imagination and vocabulary.

An Alphabet Production

Everyone gets into the act when you transform the contents of this picture book into a class play. If desired, create a backdrop resembling a stage curtain. For props, have youngsters decorate large poster-board letter cutouts. Then, in turn, have your youngsters present the alphabet letters and recite the corresponding mishaps from the book. "The B was badly Bitten."

The Z Was Zonked!

Broken! Crushed! Dropped! Eaten! Brainstorming verbs has never been so much fun! Write the letters of the alphabet on the chalkboard. Beneath each letter, write a student-generated verb beginning with that letter. If desired, repeat the activity using adjectives. Next, on scrap paper, have each youngster write a sentence about one of the alphabet letters. After the sentences have been edited, have each student copy his sentence onto a 9" x 12" sheet of colorful construction paper. Then, using a tagboard tracer, have each youngster trace his assigned letter onto the construction paper. Next have each student decorate his letter using markers, crayons, and/or construction paper scraps to reflect the action described in his sentence. Display the resulting projects in alphabetical order around the classroom.

Or, to create a class booklet, have each youngster copy his edited sentence onto a construction paper sheet. Then have him trace and decorate the corresponding letter on the blank side of the construction paper. Compile the resulting booklet pages in alphabetical order between two construction-paper covers.

The G was grabbed.

Our thanks to the following contributors to this literature feature: **Kimberly Agosta** —Substitute teacher, Raleigh, NC; **Carol Bourgeois**—Gr. 2, Buena Vista Elementary School, Greer, SC; **Tonya Byrd** —Gr. 2, Shaw Air Force Base, SC; **Tara Endris**—Gr. 2, St. Raphael School, Louisville, KY; **V. Gianakopoulos** —Librarian, Smith School Library, East Hanover, NJ; **Dawn Helton**—Gr. 3, Lumberton Primary School, Lumberton, TX; **Marilyn Leiszler**—Gr. 2, Swaney Elementary School, Derby, KS; **Darlene Marshall**—Gr. 1, South Salem School, Salem, VA; **Lynda Neuroth,** Canton, MI; **Debbie Patrick**—Gr. 3, Filbert Street Elementary, Mechanicsburg, PA; **Louise Quynn**—Media Specialist, West Elementary School, Plymouth, MA; **Kim Reding**—Gr. 2, Dallas Center–Grimes Elementary, Grimes, IA; **Judy Skalicky**—Gr. 3, Meadowbrook Elementary, Golden Valley, MN; **Kimberly Spring**—Gr. 2, Lowell Elementary School, Everett, WA; **Abby Tuch,** Oswego, NY; **Jolene Vereecke**—Gr. 1, Grandview Elementary School, Higginsville, MO; **Donna Woods**—Gr. 2, Gulf Breeze Elementary, Gulf Breeze, FL

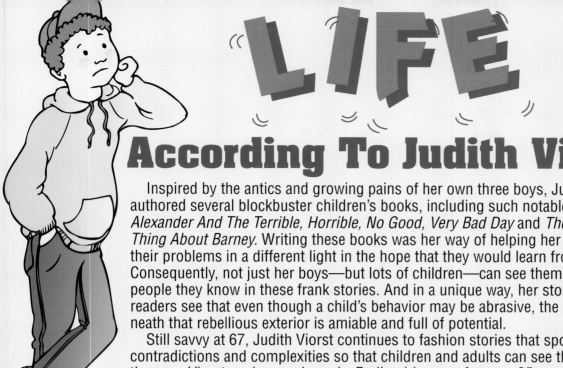

"LIFE" According To Judith Viorst

Inspired by the antics and growing pains of her own three boys, Judith Viorst authored several blockbuster children's books, including such notable favorites as *Alexander And The Terrible, Horrible, No Good, Very Bad Day* and *The Tenth Good Thing About Barney.* Writing these books was her way of helping her boys see their problems in a different light in the hope that they would learn from them. Consequently, not just her boys—but lots of children—can see themselves or people they know in these frank stories. And in a unique way, her stories help the readers see that even though a child's behavior may be abrasive, the person beneath that rebellious exterior is amiable and full of potential.

Still savvy at 67, Judith Viorst continues to fashion stories that spotlight life's contradictions and complexities so that children and adults can see them for what they are. Viorst—whose column in *Redbook* has run for over 25 years—is also a poet, novelist, and writer of adult nonfiction.

The Tenth Good Thing About Barney

Illustrated by Erik Blegvad • Published by Atheneum

In *The Tenth Good Thing About Barney,* a young boy deals with the death of his cat by recalling ten good things about this much-loved pet. Follow up the story by encouraging students to notice good things about people and things in their lives. For practice, invite each youngster to bring a stuffed toy to school and tell her classmates ten good things about her toy. Encourage students as a group to contribute at least one additional compliment about each child's stuffed critter.

Gina Parisi—Gr. 2
Demarest School
Bloomfield, NJ

Pay tribute to Barney with this "purr-fect" follow-up activity. Have students brainstorm different people and things that are beloved. List all suggestions on the chalkboard. In another column, list the positive qualities that these people and things have. Ask each student to select a person or thing from the first list and several corresponding qualities from the second list. Then, on individual lengths of adding-machine tape, have each student copy and complete this sentence: "Ten good things about [selected person or thing] are...." Show students how to curl their tapes by wrapping them around their pencils. Next have each student design a cat cutout like the one shown and attach his curled tape to the cutout so that it appears that the cat is playing with a ribbon of curly paper.

Alyssa Shulman—Gr. 3, Alief ISD, Alief, TX

Follow up a reading of *The Tenth Good Thing About Barney* by asking students to accentuate their classmates' positive qualities. Write your youngsters' names on individual slips of paper and use the slips for a student drawing. Confirm that each student received the name of a classmate; then give each youngster a brad and a construction-paper wheel and wheel cover like the ones shown. On his wheel cover, each student writes "The Tenth Good Thing About [insert the student's name from the slip drawn]." In each of the ten sections of his wheel, the student writes something positive about that person. Then, using his brad, he attaches the wheel cover atop the wheel. Ask each student to share his completed assignment. As each wheel is rotated, the child who is the subject of the project will positively light up!

Leigh Anne Newsom—Gr. 3
Greenbrier Intermediate, Chesapeake, VA

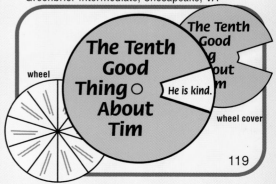

wheel

The Tenth Good Thing About Tim

The Tenth Good Thing About Tim

He is kind.

wheel cover

My Mama Says There Aren't Any Zombies, Ghosts, Vampires, Creatures, Demons, Monsters, Fiends, Goblins, Or Things

Illustrated by Kay Chorao • Published by Atheneum

The young boy in this story thinks his mother could be dead wrong when she tells him not to worry about things like ghosts and vampires. You see, he's discovered that "sometimes even mamas make mistakes"! At the conclusion of the story, talk about a variety of common fears. Then ask the youngsters to ponder their personal fears. As a writing activity, have each child write a letter to an advice columnist (such as Brave Brenda) seeking advice on dealing with a fear she has. A student can sign her real name or a make-believe name to her letter. Gather the letters; then, over the next several days, read them aloud and have the students share advice for dealing with the fears presented. Or if desired, arrange for upper-grade students to pen answers to the letters.

Mary Fernandes—Gr. 2, Village Elementary School, Syosset, NY

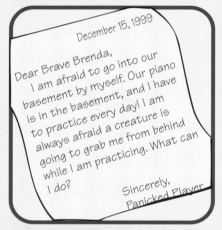

December 15, 1999

Dear Brave Brenda,
I am afraid to go into our basement by myself. Our piano is in the basement, and I have to practice every day! I am always afraid a creature is going to grab me from behind while I am practicing. What can I do?

Sincerely,
Panicked Player

Knowing that other people have fears can be reassuring to little ones. Challenge students to find out the fears their friends and relatives experience. Then have the students graph those fears on a class graph. When the graph is finished, have students identify the most (and least) common fears. Ask students to explain why certain fears are more prevalent than others. Then ask students to brainstorm ways to diminish these fears.

Mary Fernandes—Gr. 2

Rosie And Michael

Illustrated by Lorna Tomei
Published by Atheneum

When a person is your best friend, it's hard to find anyone who can top him. After reading aloud *Rosie And Michael,* your students will have a clear picture of what some friendships are like. Ask each student to design and write the text for a wanted poster that describes what he wants most in a best friend. Give students opportunities to read or listen to their classmates' descriptions.

Denise Krigger—Gr. 2, Village Elementary School, Syosset, NY

The Alphabet From Z To A (With Much Confusion On The Way)

Illustrated by Richard Hull
Published by Atheneum

Any youngster will love this irreverent scrutiny of spelling and language. But it may be of particular interest to students who have struggled with the oddities and exceptions of the English language. They will immediately relate to the points made in Judith Viorst's newest children's book, *The Alphabet From Z To A (With Much Confusion On The Way).* The book comes with a follow-up activity suggested by the author. Challenge your students—as the author does—to find for each letter the illustrations that begin with that letter. Thank goodness Viorst and Hull provided an answer key!

I'll Fix Anthony

Illustrated by Arnold Lobel
Published by Harper & Row, Publishers

A big brother like Anthony can give a little guy a complex. But Anthony's little brother is living for the glorious day when the tables will turn and he'll be more capable than Anthony. Once you've read *I'll Fix Anthony,* find out the personal improvements your students are hoping to make as they grow older. List these skills on chart paper. Beneath each listing, write students' suggestions for ways to develop these abilities. Mount the resulting poster for future inspiration.

Marni Cole—Grs. 2 & 3, Village Elementary School, Syosset, NY

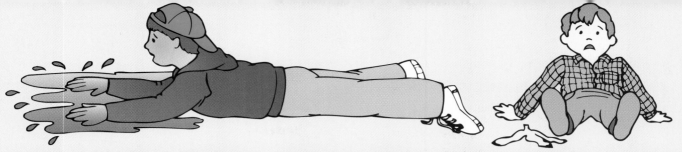

Alexander And The Terrible, Horrible, No Good, Very Bad Day

Illustrated by Ray Cruz • Published by Atheneum

Poor Alexander! In Viorst's *Alexander And The Terrible, Horrible, No Good, Very Bad Day,* he seems to be of the opinion that if he could just get to Australia, all his troubles would evaporate into thin air. Sometimes the thought of an escape or out-of-the-ordinary adventure does seem like it would be a welcomed change. Find out where each of your students would like to retreat to in the event of an especially awful day and why this prospect seems so appealing.

Carrie Winkelman—Grs. 3 & 4 Special Education, Harrison School, Omaha, NE

Challenge your students to imagine what Alexander's life would be like if he lived in Australia. Ask each student to design an Australian postcard. On the back of the postcard, have each student write a message as though he were Alexander—away from it all, at last, in Australia.

Debbie Weinheimer, Clarion, PA

We interrupt your regularly scheduled classwork to bring you this special news report. After students have had lots of time to read and reread *Alexander And The Terrible, Horrible, No Good, Very Bad Day,* pair them and ask that one child in each pair be a news reporter while the other child in the pair pretends to be Alexander. Videotape each reporter interviewing his partner to get the scoop on his catastrophic day. Once each pair has been filmed, interrupt your regularly scheduled routine to view these special news clips.

Debbie Weinheimer

Prompted by a reading of *Alexander And The Terrible, Horrible, No Good, Very Bad Day,* present this class booklet project. Have each student draw and color an incident that occurred during his all-time worst day. Then have him write an explanation of his illustration. Next help students agree upon one location that would be the perfect place to escape to—especially on a horrible day. On the last page of the class book, have one student write "Some days are like that. Even in [location of students' choice]." Compile the drawings and writings into a class booklet called "Our Terrible, Horrible, No Good, Very Bad Day." (Or if your students are more advanced, have each of them create a separate book detailing the catastrophes of his own worst day.) Whenever you notice that a student is having one of *those* days, suggest that he thumb through this latest class publication. It may help him keep his day in perspective!

Alyssa Shulman—Gr. 3, Alief ISD, Alief, TX
Linda Patten—Gr. 3, Leary Elementary School Rush, NY

Perhaps Alexander could use some advice to help him get through his very bad day. Maybe your students can remember days when everything went awry for them. Establish a panel of experts on which student volunteers take turns serving. Then have other volunteers take turns describing their bad days and their attempts to rectify the situations. Encourage the panel to put their heads together to come up with advice that could have improved each situation.

Marsha Portnoy—Grs. K-5 Reading, Village Elementary School, Syosset, NY

Alexander's day was awful. There's no disputing that. But things usually have a way of balancing out. So for all the bad days a person might have, there are usually an equal number of good days. After reading *Alexander And The Terrible, Horrible, No Good, Very Bad Day,* have students turn the tables to create stories about totally awesome days. Brainstorm with students the kinds of things that make a day wonderful. Then have each student write and illustrate her story. Provide a supply of duplicated paper strips that each read "It was a wonderful, marvelous, terrific, totally awesome day!" Each time a student wishes to incorporate this sentence into her story, she simply glues a paper strip in place. Invite students to read aloud their glowing stories for their classmates. Then, if desired, bind the stories into a class book and place it on a classroom library shelf for all to enjoy.

Eleanor Repole—Gr. 3, Kenmore Elementary School, Elkton, MD

Alexander, Who Used To Be Rich Last Sunday

Illustrated by Ray Cruz • Published by Atheneum

Alexander, Who Used To Be Rich Last Sunday is a story about a boy whose best money-saving intentions just never seem to work out. A few cents here and a few cents there, and before long Alexander is penniless. After reading *Alexander, Who Used To Be Rich Last Sunday* aloud to your students, give each youngster a dollar's worth of imitation coins as follows: seven dimes, four nickels, ten pennies. Reread the story, having students set aside an equivalent coin or set of coins each time Alexander spends some of his money. If desired, each time money is spent, pause to have students determine how much of Alexander's money still remains.

Cindy McPherson, Lee Hamilton Elementary, Ferguson, MO
Tamra Oliver—Gr. 2, Margaret Beeks Elementary, Blacksburg, VA

Money burned a hole in Alexander's pocket. Your students can probably relate to this experience. Find out what your students believe are the most challenging aspects of saving money. Encourage students to suggest ways that children can earn money too. Then ask each youngster to invent an ingenious money bank complete with devices that will keep him from spending the money that goes inside. Provide drawing supplies and have each student illustrate and write a description of the bank he has invented.

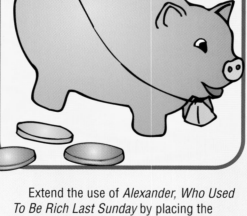

Eleanor Repole—Gr. 3, Kenmore Elementary
Elkton, MD

Extend the use of *Alexander, Who Used To Be Rich Last Sunday* by placing the book in a center along with imitation coins and a calculator. Challenge students to reread the story and determine how much money each of Alexander's brothers had. Or place imitation coins and a supply of writing paper at a center. Ask each youngster to write his own money-spending adventure.

Cindy McPherson
Tamra Oliver—Gr. 2

Earrings!

Illustrated by Nola Langner Malone
Published by Atheneum

In Judith Viorst's book *Earrings!*, a young girl laments the fact that she is not allowed to get pierced ears and earrings. Although the thought of wearing earrings completely consumes her, her parents say she'll have to wait. After reading aloud *Earrings!*, have students recall the rationales that the girl uses to justify her desire. Ask each youngster to think of something he really hoped for, but that his parent(s) wouldn't be talked into. Have the students evaluate why they felt their requests should have been granted. Also ask students to recall the antics that they used to try to convince their parents to make these purchases. Then have students write and illustrate stories about their experiences. In their stories, have them tell what they learned from their past experiences that may be helpful for future requests.

Alyssa Shulman—Gr. 3, Alief ISD, Alief, TX

After reading aloud *Earrings!*, group students into threes or fours, and have them role-play the parts of parents and children trying to resolve their differences over potential purchases. Once the role-playing has run its course, bring all the students back into a large-group discussion about what took place. Find out which methods of persuasion were most effective. Ask students to explain why they think these methods worked the best.

Wrap up your activities related to Viorst's *Earrings!* by having each student use crayons, paper scraps, scissors, assorted craft supplies, and glue to design the likeness of a person wearing one or more one-of-a-kind earrings!

Eleanor Repole—Gr. 3

A Terrific Twosome!

Begin the school year with two of the best—Audrey and Don Wood! Use these teacher-tested and student-approved activities to enhance the wonderful works of the Woods.

ideas by Jill Hamilton

Twenty-Four Robbers

Written & Illustrated by Audrey Wood
Child's Play (International) Ltd, 1980

Skillfully adapted from a traditional skipping rhyme, this playfully illustrated book will leave your children chanting for more! Twenty-four robbers make repeat visits to a cottage in the woods. The lady of the cottage graciously grants each of the robbers' requests as best she can. Just what are these robbers up to?

No doubt your youngsters will be satisfied with the tasty conclusion of this romp! After several readings of the book, invite the students to create their own soupy rhymes. Duplicate student copies of the format shown for students to complete and illustrate, or display the format and have students copy, complete, and illustrate the sentences on writing paper. Set aside time (perhaps after lunch!) for students to share their tasty creations. Then bind the rhymes into a class book titled "[class enrollment] Students!"

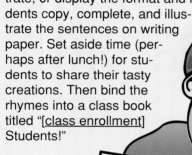

Hot ___Pickle___ Soup!
Hot ___pickle___ soup!
Hot ___pickle___ soup!
Put some ___pickles___ in the pot
And make sure it's very hot!
Add some ___mustard___ and you've got
the soup I love a lot!
Hot ___pickle___ soup!
Hot ___pickle___ soup!

The Napping House

Written by Audrey Wood & Illustrated by Don Wood
Harcourt Brace & Company, 1984

What could be more peaceful than a house where everyone is quietly napping? Maybe nothing! But as the old saying goes, nothing lasts forever. And such is the case in this cumulative tale where one wakeful flea brings down the house with just one tiny bite!

Make plans to have your class share this cumulative story with a group of parents, another classroom, or a staff member. In advance cut eight large circles from blue paper and seven large circles from yellow paper. Label each circle with a different story event. (Refer to the provided table.) Then distribute the labeled cutouts and have student pairs and/or individuals illustrate the different story events. To retell the story, have the students arrange themselves in sequential order based on the story props they've made. Then have the youngsters use their props as they retell this delightful tale. A couple of quick rehearsals and your performers will be ready for the road! Later display the props in story order on a bulletin board titled "The Napping House."

Story Events	
Blue Circles	**Yellow Circles**
a napping house	who bites the mouse
a cozy bed	who scares the cat
a snoring granny	who claws the dog
a dreaming child	who thumps the child
a dozing dog	who bumps the granny
a snoozing cat	who breaks the bed
a slumbering mouse	a napping house where
a wakeful flea	no one now is sleeping

a dozing dog

a napping house

123

Little Penguin's Tale

Written & Illustrated by Audrey Wood
Harcourt Brace Jovanovich, Publishers; 1989
When Granny Nanny Penguin begins a story for seven little penguins, one little penguin wanders away. As Granny Nanny relates each exciting episode of her story, the seventh little penguin encounters the very same adventure in his travels—right down to landing in the mouth of a whale!

Sometimes when we make mistakes, there is physical evidence that we shouldn't have done what we did. The penguin's missing tail feathers were a good example of this! Ask students to recall mistakes they've made that yielded physical results. Examples might include a skinned knee that resulted from running instead of walking, or a broken leg that resulted from climbing a tree that was off-limits. Then give each child a tan cutout that resembles a self-adhesive bandage. In the center section have each child draw a picture that illustrates the mistake that he made. In the remaining spaces have the student write (or dictate for you to write) what he learned from the illustrated incident.

I burned my fingers on a pot of fudge pudding. My mom said the pudding was hot.

She said not to touch it. I learned that my mom knew what she was talking about!

Little Penguin couldn't resist dancing with the gooney birds and your students won't be able to resist making one!

For each gooney bird you will need:

a 1" Styrofoam® ball	two wiggle eyes
a 2" Styrofoam® ball	colorful craft feathers
two 6" lengths of pipe cleaner	glue
a 3" length of pipe cleaner	scissors
a 3" square of red or orange poster board	tape

To make the head:
1. Glue the two wiggle eyes to the smaller Styrofoam® ball.
2. Cut a small diamond shape from the poster board and insert one point of the resulting beak into the ball.
3. Glue craft feathers to the head as desired.

To make the body:
1. Insert the two 6" lengths of pipe cleaner (legs) into the bottom of the larger Styrofoam® ball.
2. Cut two foot shapes from the poster board.
3. Tape one foot cutout to the bottom of each pipe-cleaner leg.
4. Glue craft feathers to the body as desired.

To assemble the project:
1. Use the 3" length of pipe cleaner (neck) to join the head and body.
2. Bend the pipe-cleaner legs and neck to achieve a desired look.

Tooth Fairy

Written & Illustrated by Audrey Wood
Child's Play (International) Ltd, 1985

Jealous because her brother lost a tooth and she didn't, Jessica tries to trick the tooth fairy with a painted kernel of corn. But, as Jessica finds out, you can't trick the tooth fairy. She also learns that tooth fairies are very forgiving and extremely smart!

Youngsters may say they don't believe in the tooth fairy, but that doesn't mean they'll pass up the chance to put a lost tooth under their pillows—just in case! And the thought of having a tooth displayed in the Hall Of Perfect Teeth is just too good to be true! Follow up this fanciful story by reviewing good dental health habits with your class. Then ask each child to complete a copy of page 128. At the end of the day, send each child home with her tips for keeping healthy teeth and a white kernel of pop-corn. Suggest that each child use these two items to retell Jessica's story to a family member. "Loose Tooth Away!"

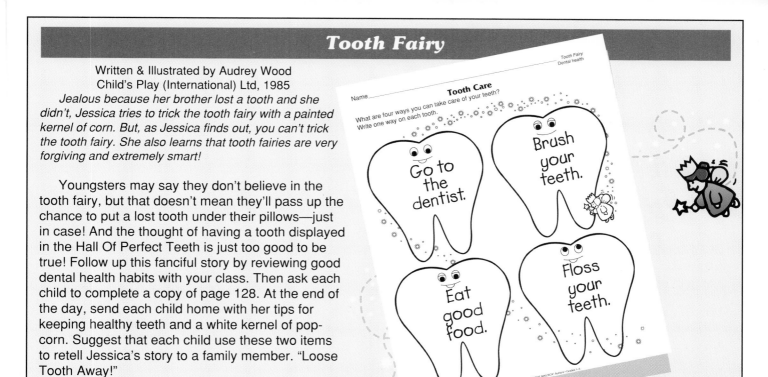

The Little Mouse, The Red Ripe Strawberry, And The Big Hungry Bear

Written by Don and Audrey Wood
Illustrated by Don Wood
Child's Play (International) Ltd, 1993

If a big hungry bear can smell a picked, red, ripe straw-berry from a mile away, how is a tiny little mouse supposed to keep his picked strawberry a secret? If hiding it, guard-ing it, and disguising it won't do, there is another possibility that should work quite nicely!

There's a good chance that this kid-pleasing book will make your youngsters hungry for strawberries! Here's a simple treat that's sure to quench their cravings. To serve between 25 and 30 youngsters, stir two quarts of sliced strawberries into four quarts of strawberry yogurt. Spoon the mixture into indi-vidual plastic cups. Then give each child a graham cracker inside a plastic sandwich bag, a serving of strawberry dessert, and a spoon. Remind students about the big hungry bear, and suggest that they dis-guise their strawberries just in case the bear is nearby. To do this, have each child crumble the cracker inside the plastic bag, then sprinkle the re-sulting crumbs on top of his strawberry dessert. Invite students to eat their treats, all the while keeping their eyes open for that big hungry bear!

The adorable mouse featured in the book never says a word. But a quick look at the illustrations re-veals that the mouse has plenty on its mind! Page back through the book, allowing students to study each double-spread illustration. Ask students to share their ideas for what the mouse might have said each time it was featured. For each page, help the class choose one mouse-related comment. Copy this comment on an individual sticky note. Trim the note to resemble a speech balloon and attach it to the corresponding page in the book. Then reread the book for your students, this time reading aloud the mouse's comments as well as the authors' words.

125

Weird Parents

Written & Illustrated by Audrey Wood
Dial Books For Young Readers, 1990
This wildly funny and most affectionate story expresses what most youngsters feel about their parents at one time or another—no matter how embarrassing parents can sometimes be, they are still greatly loved.

If you're planning to invite your students' parents to school for Open House or another classroom event, follow up your reading of *Weird Parents* with this activity. Have each child think of one weird thing that an adult in his family does, like singing in the shower, kissing children in public, or wearing totally uncool shoes. Then have each student illustrate a parent or guardian doing something weird. One-sentence descriptions may be added below the illustrations, but no names should be included. Display the completed projects on a bulletin board titled "Our Parents: They May Do Weird Stuff, But We Love Them Just The Same!" Also display Audrey Wood's book nearby. Your visitors are sure to have a good laugh as they peruse this one-of-a-kind attraction.

Students will also enjoy comparing and contrasting the family featured in *Weird Parents* with the prehistoric family from *The Tickleoctopus* (featured on this page). Record the student-generated information on a large Venn diagram that you've drawn on the chalkboard. Next challenge students to write and illustrate stories about a time when these two similar—but uniquely different—families meet. You can count on a batch of really *weird* stories that will *tickle* everyone's funny bones!

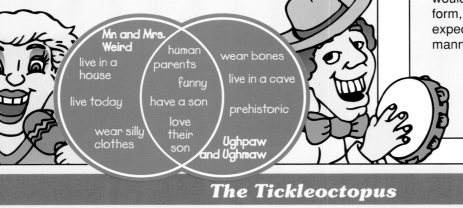

Mr. and Mrs. Weird
- live in a house
- live today
- wear silly clothes

human parents
funny
have a son
love their son

- wear bones
- live in a cave
- prehistoric
- Ughpaw and Ughmaw

Rude Giants

Written & Illustrated by Audrey Wood
Harcourt Brace Jovanovich, Publishers; 1993
Beatrix the butter maid and Gerda the cow have some colossal problems when two rude giants move close by. But even giants can be taught manners—when their teachers are Beatrix and Gerda!

When youngsters learn that the baby giant is even more rude than its once-rude parents, they'll be flabbergasted! Find out what kinds of behavior your students think could earn the baby this reputation. List their ideas on one half of a piece of bulletin-board paper. Next have the students brainstorm creative ways for Beatrix and Gerda to cure the youngster of each ill manner listed. Write these ideas on the remaining half of the paper. If desired, leave the resulting poster on display and encourage students to write and illustrate reform tales titled "Rude Baby Giant." This would also be a perfect time to inform, discuss, and/or review your expectations concerning classroom manners.

The Tickleoctopus

Written by Audrey Wood & Illustrated by Don Wood
Harcourt Brace & Company, 1994
According to this tale, prehistoric families were downright miserable until a young caveboy named Bup discovered the tickleoctopus. So what is a tickleoctopus? You'll have to read this delightful story to find out!

So what does a tickleoctopus look like? Even though only the long, pink arms of this extraordinary creature are revealed, you can count on your youngsters having some ideas about what the tickleoctopus looks like in its entirety! Provide time for students to either illustrate their creations on drawing paper, or mold them from generous portions of pink play dough. Then, as each child shares his creation with his classmates, ask him to tell how he plans to put his tickleoctopus to use!

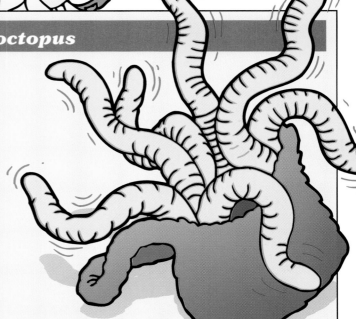

Quick As A Cricket

Written by Audrey Wood & Illustrated by Don Wood
Child's Play (International) Ltd, 1995
In this joyful celebration of self-awareness a young boy compares himself to a variety of living creatures. The rhythmic use of similes and the captivating illustrations make this slim paperback an appealing choice for any audience.

Learning how students perceive themselves can provide you with valuable insight into your new class! Read the story aloud a second time. Follow up each simile by inviting students to tell about times that they have felt as the boy describes. Conclude your second reading by recognizing that each class member has many traits, just as the boy in the story does. Next ask each student to choose a simile from the story or create one of his own that he thinks best describes himself. On one side of a white construction-paper circle, have each student write (or dictate for you to write) his self-selected simile. Then have each student illustrate and personalize his simile on the blank side of his circle. To complete his project, a student hole-punches the top of his cutout, threads a length of yarn (or curling ribbon) through the hole, securely ties the yarn ends, and dangles the resulting medallion from his neck. Now look who's feeling as proud as a peacock!

I'm as fast as a cheetah!

Adrian

The Bunyans

Written by Audrey Wood
Illustrated by David Shannon
The Blue Sky Press, 1996
Paul Bunyan a family man? That's right! In this rollicking extension of Paul Bunyan's story, readers meet Paul's wife and his two enormous children. It's a family your youngsters won't soon forget!

Boy, those Bunyans had busy "younguns"! At the conclusion of this far-fetched tale, enlist your students' help in locating on a map of the United States the natural wonders that the Bunyan children created. Next write a student-generated list of other natural wonders these "younguns" might have also created. Then, working in small groups, in pairs, or individually, have the students write and illustrate far-fetched tales that feature the Bunyan children creating more natural wonders. Have students work on large-size paper; then bind the projects into a one-of-a-kind *big* book.

The Red Racer

Written & Illustrated by Audrey Wood
Simon & Schuster Books For Young Readers, 1996
Nona wants a new bike and it can't be just any new bike! The new bike must be a Deluxe Red Racer. But Nona's parents refuse to buy her a new bike because she already has a bike that she can ride. So what does this spunky heroine do? She schemes to get rid of her junky old bike! It seems like a perfect plan until…

This high-energy story provides the perfect opportunity to talk about *needs* and *wants*. Write the terms on the chalkboard and enlist your students' help in defining each one. After students have defined *needs* as things a consumer must have to stay alive and *wants* as things that make a consumer's life easier, ask students to categorize Nona's desire for a new bike. Also find out if your students think Nona's parents had additional reasons for not buying the new bike. In conclusion, discuss how everyone ended up being happy, even though everyone didn't get exactly what he or she wished for. If time allows, invite students to share or write about experiences that they have had that were similar to Nona's.

Tooth Care

What are four ways you can take care of your teeth?
Write one way on each tooth.

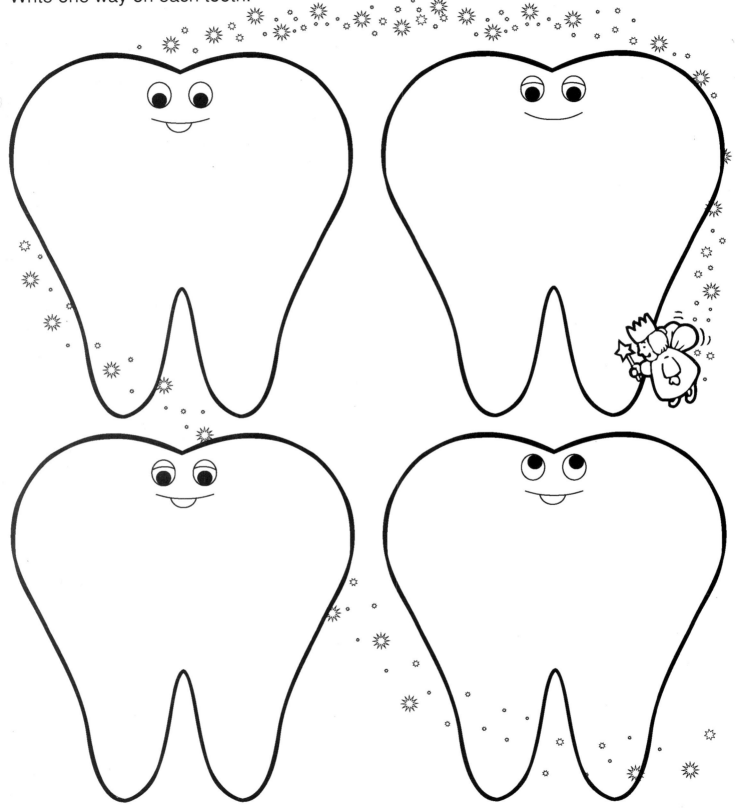

Note To Teacher: Use this page with *Tooth Fairy* on page 125.